VISITORS FROM SPACE
The Fellowship of Golden Illumination

Eugene H. Drake

SAUCERIAN PUBLISHER

ISBN: **9781736731499**

© **2022, Saucerian Publisher**

TABLE OF CONTENTS

Eugene Harry Drake: The first contactee that nobody knows

It is generally a good idea to return to the classics in any genre. This also goes for UFO literature. Rereading a book, or reviewing old documents after ten or twenty years is a rewarding experience. You will discover new data and ideas you didn´t notice before. The reason, of course, is that you are, in many ways, not the same person reading the book the second or third time. Hopefully you have advanced in knowledge, experience, intellectual and spiritual discernment.

California has been the melting pot and breeding ground, where the ingredients of what would come to be known as the New Age were melted and mixed. Here, this was where the spirit mediums entered in contact with beings from space. The forerunners of the flying saucers were the Foo Fighters which appeared during the Second World War. Then, they were replaced by the "flying disk." The new emerging religious sects leaders created an eclectic product that would give way to a new religion: Saucerism.

Saucerism is the assumptions and approaches adopted by members of the contactee cults and their leaders: the discourse, ideology construction, and social organization of contactee groups. In constructing the theological worldview of these contactees, cult evolved from the New Age and New Pagan movement, its broader interest in ufology, extraterrestrial life, and alien visitation. Also, it postulates a series of close encounters with alien visitations that are a kind of "angelnauts". Borrowing from its ufological origins, the theology assumes that extraterrestrials are interested in assisting human beings to spiritual self-improvement, self-transformation, and technological development to higher levels. A cult leader, acting as a "prophet" who has the gift of communicating with the angelnauts, who thinks that he has been misinterpreted during his lifetime due to his advanced ways of thinking about society, he is the key figure in these cults. In essence, these contactee prophets are like Jesus Christ that was misunderstood, rejected and not received by the world. The "prophet" is the "chosen one" by the angelnauts to receive the E.T revelations for his/hers (mostly his) extraordinary gift and advance spiritual development. These prophets had acquired knowledge "beyond our understanding". They claim that the world would experience a "great spiritual awakening" with the arrival of the angelnauts, and human society will never move forward as long as the "angelnauts" do not cooperate with earthlings. The prophecized a new age of enlightenment humans with greater intelligence created with the help of angelnauts. In the long run, Saucerism lies at the roots of the biblical scriptures to support the ideology construct.

Not too much is known about Drake's work and his whereabouts. He was not a prolific author (he only published two booklets of 38 and 34 pages, respectively: *Visitors from Space: Space Ships, Discs, Flying Saucers* (no publication date given, but probably 1949 or 1950); *Life On the Planets. A visit to Venus (1950)*. Both titles were published under the banner of Drake's The Fellowship of Golden Illumination), nor did he get much publicity like George Adamski or George Van Tassel. He did not appear in flying saucer congress like Van Tassel's Giant Rock

Interplanetary Space Convention, nor did he appear on TV or radio programs. Little is known of Drake. However, based on his few publications, he was the Director of a private organization called: The Fellowship of Golden Illumination located in Los Angeles, California (1014 South Lake Street).

Google's Map Street View (Nov, 2021) of 1014 South Lake Street in Los Angeles, California

The question is whether Drake was plagiarized or taken as a role-model by subsequent contactees. We said that the contactees who preceded him plagiarized his work. However, the most plausible explanation is that Drake was the forerunner, instigator, or inspiration for the contactees who preceded him, like George Adamski and others. For example: Van Tassel's Council of the Seven Lights, published in 1958, is very similar to Drake's *Visitors from Space: Space Ships, Discs, Flying Saucers*, published around 1949-1950.

Eugene Harry Drake was born 22 September 1889 (or 1888, maybe in 1888 and registered one year later) in Triumph, Warren County, Pennsylvania, to Zachariah Taylor Drake and Sarah Jane (Jackson). His father worked as a Pumper Oil. Drake was the only son of five children. He had four sisters: Merna Z Drake (1885); Edna E Drake (1886); Mary Drake (1890); Maud Drake (1892).

Eugene H. Drake 1951. Taken from Håkan Blomqvist (2017)

Eugene Drake and family 1920s. Taken from Håkan Blomqvist (2017)

❧ancestry

Eugene Harry Drake
BIRTH 22 SEP 1889 • Triumph Township, Warren, Warren, Pennsylvania, USA
DEATH 21 FEB 1973 • Santa Monica, Los Angeles, California, USA

Facts

Age 0 — Birth
22 Sep 1889 • Triumph Township, Warren, Warren, Pennsylvania, USA

Birth of sister Mary Ann Elizabeth Drake-Wooster-Nelson (1890–1972)
04 May 1890 • Triumph Township, Warren, Pennsylvania, USA

Age 1 — Birth of sister Bessie May Drake (1891–)
Jan 1891 • Triumph Township, Warren, Pennsylvania, USA

Age 2 — Birth of sister Maude Elizabeth Drake (1892–1970)
30 Apr 1892 • Triumph Township, Warren, Pennsylvania

Age 6 — Death of mother Sarah Jane Jackson (1860–1896)
14 Aug 1896 • Triumph, Warren, Pennsylvania, USA

Age 25 — Marriage
3 Jun 1915 • Los Angeles, California, USA
Priscilla Atlee Putnam (1891–1982)

Age 26 — Birth of daughter Priscilla Eugenia Drake-Forsyth (1916–1982)
18 Jun 1916 • Los Angeles County, California, USA

Age 27 — Birth of daughter Irene Atlee Drake (1917–2016)
08 Aug 1917 • Los Angeles, Los Angeles, California, USA

Age 29 — Death of father Zachariah Taylor Drake (1848–1919)
08 May 1919 • Triumph, Warren, Pennsylvania, USA

Age 31 — Residence
1920 • Santa Monica, Los Angeles, California, USA
Relation to Head: Head; Residence Marital Status: Married

Age 38 — Residence
1927 • Santa Monica, California, USA

Age 39 — Residence
1928 • Santa Monica, California, USA

Family

Parents

Zachariah Taylor Drake
1848–1919

Sarah Jane Jackson
1860–1896

Spouse & Children

Priscilla Atlee Putnam
1891–1982

Priscilla Eugenia Drake-Forsyth
1916–1982

Irene Atlee Drake
1917–2016

Sources

Ancestry Sources

1920 United States Federal Census

1930 United States Federal Census

1940 United States Federal Census

Ancestry Family Trees

California, County Birth, Marriage, and Death Records, 1849-1980

California, Death Index, 1940-1997

U.S. City Directories, 1822-1995

U.S. City Directories, 1822-1995

Age 41 — **Residence**
1930 • Santa Monica, Los Angeles, California
Marital Status: Married; Relation to Head of House: Head

Age 46 — **Residence**
1935 • New York, New York

Age 50 — **Residence**
1 Apr 1940 • Santa Monica, Los Angeles, California, USA
Marital Status: Married; Relation to Head of House: Head

Age 53 — **Residence**
1942 • Santa Monica, California

Age 67 — **Death of brother William Harrison (Harry) Drake** (1888–1956)
29 Oct 1956 • Titusville, Crawford, Pennsylvania, USA

Age 77 — **Death of sister Myrna Zatella Drake** (1885–1966)
13 Oct 1966 • Warren, Warren, Pennsylvania, USA

Age 80 — **Death of sister Maude Elizabeth Drake** (1892–1970)
04 Aug 1970 • Erie, Erie County, Pennsylvania, USA

Age 83 — **Death of sister Mary Ann Elizabeth Drake-Wooster- Nelson** (1890–1972)
1 Dec 1972 • Youngsville, Warren County, Pennsylvania, USA

Age 83 — **Death**
21 Feb 1973 • Santa Monica, Los Angeles, California, USA

Residence
Pasadena, Los Angeles, California, USA
Military Marital Status: Married

U.S. General Land Office Records, 1776-2015

U.S., Social Security Death Index, 1935-2014

U.S., World War I Draft Registration Cards, 1917-1918

U.S., World War II Draft Registration Cards, 1942

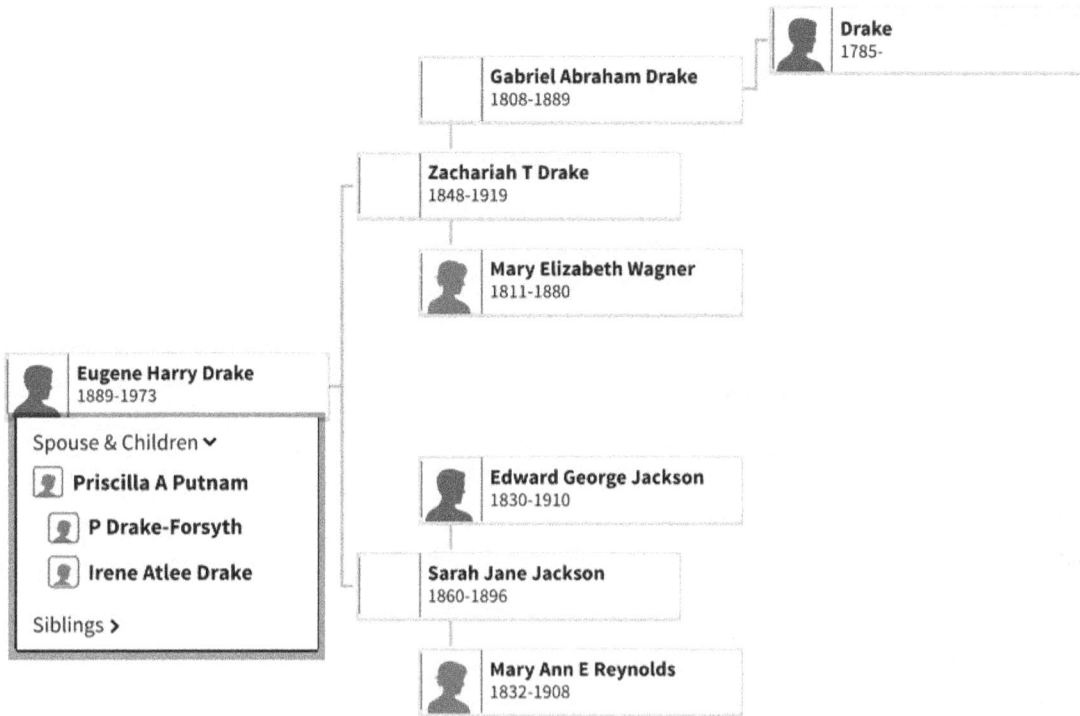

Eugene Harry Drake
1889-1973

Spouse & Children ⌄

👤 **Priscilla A Putnam**

  👤 **P Drake-Forsyth**

  👤 **Irene Atlee Drake**

Siblings ❯

Zachariah T Drake
1848-1919

Gabriel Abraham Drake
1808-1889

Drake
1785-

Mary Elizabeth Wagner
1811-1880

Sarah Jane Jackson
1860-1896

Edward George Jackson
1830-1910

Mary Ann E Reynolds
1832-1908

Priscilla Atlee Putnam

BIRTH 19 JUL 1891 • Worcester, Worcester, Massachusetts, USA
DEATH 01 AUG 1982 • Los Angeles, Los Angeles, California, USA

Facts

Age 0 — Birth
19 Jul 1891 • Worcester, Worcester, Massachusetts, USA

Age 9 — Residence
1900 • Worcester Ward 7, Worcester, Massachusetts, USA
Marital Status: Single; Relation to Head: Daughter

Age 19 — Residence
1910 • Worcester Ward 10, Worcester, Massachusetts, USA
Marital Status: Single; Relation to Head of House: Daughter

Age 23 — Marriage
3 Jun 1915 • Los Angeles, California, USA

Eugene Harry Drake
(1889–1973)

Age 24 — Birth of daughter Priscilla Eugenia Drake-Forsyth (1916–1982)
18 Jun 1916 • Los Angeles County, California, USA

Age 25 — Death of father William "Atlee" Putnam (1862–1917)
9 Jan 1917 • Los Angeles, California, USA

Age 26 — Birth of daughter Irene Atlee Drake (1917–2016)
08 Aug 1917 • Los Angeles, Los Angeles, California, USA

Age 29 — Residence
1920 • Santa Monica, Los Angeles, California, USA
Relation to Head: Wife; Residence Marital Status: Married

Age 36 — Residence
1927 • Santa Monica, California, USA

Age 37 — Residence
1928 • Santa Monica, California, USA

Age 39 — Residence
1930 • Santa Monica, Los Angeles, California
Marital Status: Married; Relation to Head of House: Wife

Age 44 — Residence
1935 • Santa Monica, Los Angeles, California

Family

Parents

William "Atlee" Putnam
1862–1917

Mary "Jennie" Donaldson
1858–1939

Spouse & Children

Eugene Harry Drake
1889–1973

Priscilla Eugenia Drake-Forsyth
1916–1982

Irene Atlee Drake
1917–2016

Sources

Ancestry Sources

1900 United States Federal Census

1910 United States Federal Census

1920 United States Federal Census

1930 United States Federal Census

1940 United States Federal Census

Ancestry Family Trees

California, County Birth, Marriage, and Death Records, 1849-1980

California, Death Index, 1940-1997

Age 47 — **Residence**
1938 • Los Angeles, California, USA

Age 48 — **Death of mother Mary "Jennie" Donaldson** (1858–1939)
02 Dec 1939 • Rutland, Worcester, Massachusetts, USA

Age 48 — **Residence**
1 Apr 1940 • Santa Monica, Los Angeles, California, USA
Marital Status: Married; Relation to Head of House: Wife

Age 81 — **Death of husband Eugene Harry Drake** (1889–1973)
21 Feb 1973 • Santa Monica, Los Angeles, California, USA

Age 91 — **Death**
01 Aug 1982 • Los Angeles, Los Angeles, California, USA

California, Voter Registrations, 1900-1968

Massachusetts, Town and Vital Records, 1620-1988

U.S. City Directories, 1822-1995

U.S. City Directories, 1822-1995

U.S., Social Security Death Index, 1935-2014

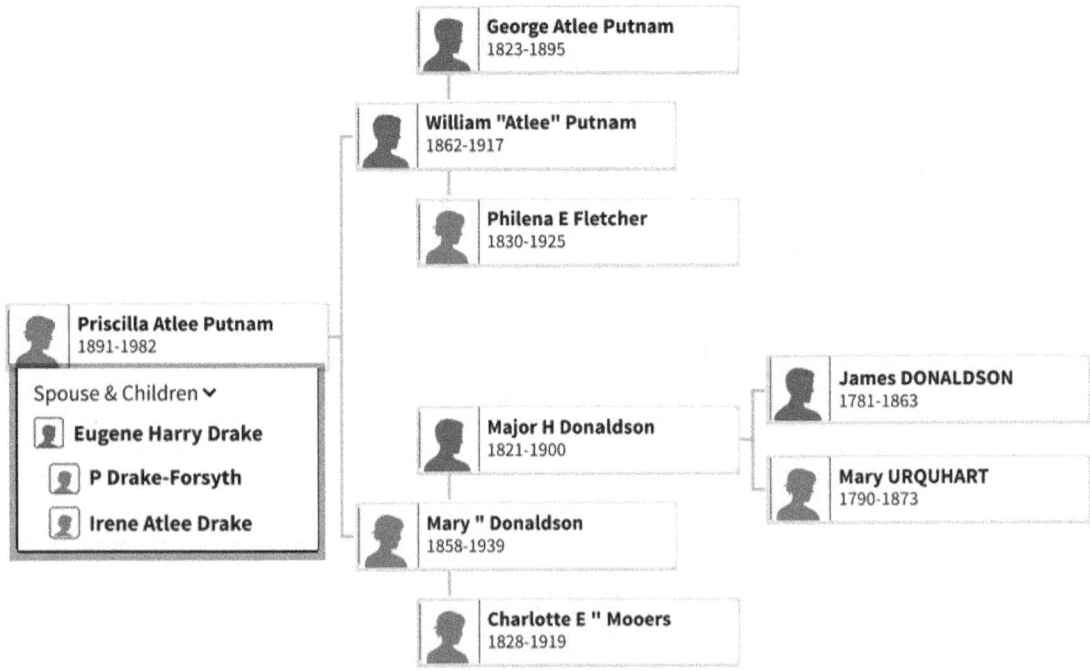

George Atlee Putnam
1823-1895

William "Atlee" Putnam
1862-1917

Philena E Fletcher
1830-1925

Priscilla Atlee Putnam
1891-1982

Spouse & Children ⌄

Eugene Harry Drake

P Drake-Forsyth

Irene Atlee Drake

Major H Donaldson
1821-1900

James DONALDSON
1781-1863

Mary URQUHART
1790-1873

Mary " Donaldson
1858-1939

Charlotte E " Mooers
1828-1919

By 1900, Drake was living with his family at Triumph, Warren County, Pennsylvania. He relocated to Southern California around 1912. There is a California, U.S., Voter Registrations listing that may have been him but was going by the name of Eugene H. Drake. This person was registered as a Republican voter, living at 1012 Wilde St in L.A. County.

On June 3, 1915 (Los Angeles, California), he married Priscilla Atlee Putnam, AKA; Priscilla Putnam, AKA; Priscilla Drake (father: W. A. Putnam, mother: Tessie D. Putnam). Putnam was born on July 19, 1891, in Worcester, Massachusetts. The couple had two daughters born in California: Priscilla E. Drake (born in 1917) & Irene A. Drake (born in 1918).

According to Drake's U.S., World War I Draft Registration Cards (1917-1918), in 1917, He worked with the New England Life Insurance Company in Los Angeles. Also, he was Private artillery with the New Jersey and California national guards. However, he did not serve in World War I.

During 1920, Drake lived in Santa Monica, California, and worked as a manager in the film exchange industry. His mother-in-law, Mary "Jennie" Donaldson, lived with them. On December 2, 1939, she died in Rutland, Worcester, Massachusetts.

By 1923 he was working as a bookkeeper, and by 1927 as a salesman. In 1927, his residence was at Wilshire Blvd in Santa Monica, California.

By 1930, Eugene H. Drake lived at 1435 Euclid Street in Santa Monica, California. He worked as a salesman of building materials. In the 1940s, he lived at 2503 Fourth Street in Santa Monica with his wife, a granddaughter (Christina A Leseberg), and a daughter: Irene A Leseberg, AKA: Irene A Drake. Drake was a worker in private work.

According to Drake's 1942 U.S. World War II Draft Registration Cards, he lived in Santa Monica, California.

In 1948, he may have been living in Bell City, California. There is a Dr. Eugene H. Drake in the city's directory listing. It is unknown if the Doctoral degree was earned honorific. In of November of that year, he was advertised as teaching a series of Thursday classes at the Universal Truth Church in Long Beach. The subject was not stated in the newspaper ads (Joshua Blu (2016). Cited by Håkan Blomqvist (2017).

The 1956 California, U.S., Voter Registrations listing has one Eugene H Drake as a Republican voter living at 6834 Woodward Ave in L.A. County. By 1962, the C.A. Voter List reported him living at 6324 Otis Ave in the same county and registered as a Republican voter. It seems that both individuals are the same.

By 1950's he started attending conventions, and putting out his books and magazine. On the 8th of September, 1957, Drake attended the "first Spacecraft Picnic" sponsored by the editor of Understanding Magazine, Daniel Fry, at Alhambra, California. There is no other reference on this "Spacecraft Picnic. Also, there are no descriptions of the kind of activities there. However,

Eugene H Drake

in the California, U.S., County Birth, Marriage, and Death Records, 1849-1980

View

Add or update information

Name:	Eugene H Drake
Gender:	Male
Event Type:	Marriage
Marriage Date:	3 Jun 1915
Marriage Place:	Los Angeles, California, USA
Spouse:	Priscilla Putnam

Suggested Record

- 1920 United States Fe
  Eugene H Drake
- 1930 United States Fe
  Eugene H Drake
- 1940 United States Fe
  Eugene H Drake

14 245	30	Preluzsky	Elsie	Jack Posner	6842	225	236
04 262	Dec 9	Prentice	Laura M.	Wm. W. McClellan	7084	229	210
15 120	21	Pratt	Jessie I.	James P. Chase	7231	230	61
07 13	24	Pratt	Edna M.	Horley A. Pockord	7186	234	81
09 39	Jan. 4	Price	Jessie M.	Thomas E Springer	7550	230	156
06 237	7	Prioleau	Bessie	Nathaniel Campbell	46	231	129
16 254	5	Prevost	Harriet W.	Herbert A. Poage	94	230	212
16 292	Feb 1	Psenner	Kathryn M.	Lewis P. Johnson	464	230	340
19 84	2	Priddy	Ida J.	James T. Johnson	454	231	277
18 209	23	Price	Amy D.	Frank Cameron	834	233	139
08 240	Apr. 12	Preble	Harriet O.	Jessie W. Park	1625	235	96
19 233	13	Pumphrey	Virginia A.	Roy L. Swinney	1434	234	348
11 26	May 7	Price	Lily M.	Leslie Phillips	2653	236	178
11 74	21	"	Gertrude M.	Wm. H. Bradshaw	2328	238	9
11 75	25	Prescott	Helen B.	Bernard H. Linden	2327	238	58
11 131	26	Pyne	Myrtle R.	Herbert C. Wilton	2372	238	43
12 142	29	Pyles	Charity D.	Adolphus G. Hinckley	2510	238	61
12 191	Jun 2	Pratt	Hazel A.	Augustus Ellsworth	2453	235	93
14 48	3	Putnam	Priscilla	Eugene H. Drake	2482	236	215
13 112	11	Prentiss	Mildred V.	Wm. C. Scharman	2760	238	171
14 91	11	Prunzel	Elsie J.	Pero Bojalo	2802	238	172
13 256	14	Pumphrey	Myrtle A	Joseph A. Peters	2536	239	55
15 281	15	Price	Maud E.	Chauncey P. Wright	6294	238	212
17 98	21	Prewitt	Florence R.	Gordon D. Roberts	2543	239	122
15 91	22	Pruett	Ivy	Vincent McGee	2959	238	268
17 215	24	Puschner	Vera J.	Arthur L. Bell	2933	238	526
17 236	Jul 12	Prout	Alice K.	Stanton R. Cutler	3519	241	69
12 229	14	Pryor	Frances	Andrea Borgia	3611	241	94
16 300	19	Purdie	Martha M.	Fred E. Platten	3654	239	331
11 82	30	Priest	Florence A.	Marcus W. Cook	3865	241	265

REGISTRATION CARD

Form 1 8 23 No. 3 (Three)

1	Name in full _Eugene Harry Drake_ (Given name) (Family name)	Age, in yrs. 27

2 Home address _531 North Lake Pasadena Cal_
(No.) (Street) (City) (State)

3 Date of birth _Sep't 22nd 1889_
(Month) (Day) (Year)

4 Are you (1) a natural-born citizen, (2) a naturalized citizen, (3) an alien, (4) or have you declared your intention (specify which)? _Natural-born citizen_

5 Where were you born? _Langhorne Penn. U.S._
(Town) (State) (Nation)

6 If not a citizen, of what country are you a citizen or subject? ____

7 What is your present trade, occupation, or office? _Cashier of New Eng. Mut. L.I.C._

8 By whom employed? _New Eng Mutual Life Ins. Co_
Where employed? _515 Citizens Nat'l Bank Bldg. Los Angeles_

9 Have you a father, mother, wife, child under 12, or a sister or brother under 12, solely dependent on you for support (specify which)? _Wife and child One yr. old._

10 Married or single (which)? _Married_ Race (specify which)? _Caucasian_

11 What military service have you had? Rank _Private_ ; branch _Infantry_
years _2 yrs_ ; Nation or State _New Jersey_

12 Do you claim exemption from draft (specify grounds)? _As a man of family_

I affirm that I have verified above answers and that they are true.

Also 3 yrs. as Private Artillery in California

Eugene Harry Drake
(Signature or mark)

If person is of African descent, tear off this corner

Drake's U.S., World War I Draft Registration Cards, (1917-1918)

REGISTRAR'S REPORT

1 | Tall, medium, or short (specify which)? _Tall_   Slender, medium, or stout (which)? _Medium_

2 | Color of eyes? _Brown_   Color of hair? _Dark brown_   Bald? _No_

3 | Has person lost arm, leg, hand, foot, or both eyes, or is he otherwise disabled (specify)? _Not disabled in any way._

I certify that my answers are true, that the person registered has read his own answers, that I have witnessed his signature, and that all of his answers of which I have knowledge are true, except as follows:

Blanche B Harold
(Signature of registrar)

Precinct _40_

City or County _Pasadena, Los Angeles –_

State _California_   _June 5 - 1917_
(Date of registration)

Drake's U.S., World War I Draft Registration Cards, (1917-1918)

REGISTRATION CARD—(Men born on or after April 28, 1877 and on or before February 16, 1897)

SERIAL NUMBER	1. NAME (Print)			ORDER NUMBER
U 2099	EUGENE	HARRY	DRAKE	
	(First)	(Middle)	(Last)	

2. PLACE OF RESIDENCE (Print)   APT 4.
2503 - 4TH ST.   SANTA MONICA   L.A   CALIF.

(Number and street) — (Town, township, village, or city) — (County) — (State)

[THE PLACE OF RESIDENCE GIVEN ON THE LINE ABOVE WILL DETERMINE LOCAL BOARD JURISDICTION; LINE 2 OF REGISTRATION CERTIFICATE WILL BE IDENTICAL]

3. MAILING ADDRESS

SAME

[Mailing address if other than place indicated on line 2. If same insert word same]

4. TELEPHONE	5. AGE IN YEARS	6. PLACE OF BIRTH
S.M. 62687	52	HANGHORNE
	DATE OF BIRTH	(Town or county)
	SEPT 22 1889	PENN.
(Exchange) (Number)	(Mo.) (Day) (Yr.)	(State or country)

7. NAME AND ADDRESS OF PERSON WHO WILL ALWAYS KNOW YOUR ADDRESS   APT. 5
MRS. BEVERLY FORSYTH   2503 - 4TH ST. SANTA MONICA, CALIF.

8. EMPLOYER'S NAME AND ADDRESS
NONE

9. PLACE OF EMPLOYMENT OR BUSINESS

(Number and street or R.F.D. number) — (Town) — (County) — (State)

I AFFIRM THAT I HAVE VERIFIED ABOVE ANSWERS AND THAT THEY ARE TRUE.

Eugene Harry Drake

D. S. S. Form 1
(Revised 4-1-42)   (over)   16-21630-2   (Registrant's signature)

U.S., World War II Draft Registration Card, 1942 for Eugene Harry Drake

14

Eugene Harry Drake
in the U.S., World War I Draft Registration Cards, 1917-1918

Detail	Source
Name:	Eugene Harry Drake
Race:	Caucasian (White)
Marital Status:	Married
Birth Date:	22 Sep 1889
Birth Place:	Pennsylvania, USA
Residence Date:	1917-1918
Street Address:	539 West Lake
Residence Place:	Pasadena, Los Angeles, California, USA
Draft Board:	1
Physical Build:	Medium
Height:	Tall
Hair Color:	Dark Brown
Eye Color:	Brown

Provi
Recor

Sug

1
Eu

1
Eu

1
Eu

C

it is possible that lectures were given to the 300 attendees. But this was a small crowd for Eugene Drake to make himself known.

BULLETIN BOARD

The first Spacecraft Picnic sponsored by Understanding in Alhambra on September 8th has been acclaimed a success. There were about 300 friends and members in attendance. Representatives of UFO Clubs and Units were on hand from L.A., Pomona, Vista, Long Beach, Ventura, Redwood City, Fontana, San Fernando, Orange and El Monte. Among the guests were Dana Howard, Calvin Girvin, **Eugene Drake** *and Eloise Mellor and many other leaders in the New Age Movement.*

We wish to welcome Orange County Spacecraft Club as Unit No. 7 of understanding. We hear they have a fine group in Orange and know that we will be receiving good reports from them.

Mr. A. G. Rose has been elected president of the Vista Unit for the year 57-58, replacing Mrs. Martha Sheppard who has done a wonderful job of organizing and expanding.

Unit No. 6 of San Fernando held an interesting meeting on September 28th with Dana Howard as guest speaker. Mr. Frank Spiva, Assistant Editor of Understanding and author of "America Know Thy Destiny," will be their speaker for November 8th. For exact. time and location contact Charlotte Sullivan, 3414 North San Fernando Rd., Burbank, Calif.

Unit No. 1 of El Monte will present the motion picture "The Day the Earth Stood Still" on Saturday, October 19th. 7:30 and 0:00 P.M. at 517 Stewart St., El Monte, Calif. Tickets may be obtained from Understanding, 11376 Frankmont St., El Monte. Proceeds from these presentations will apply toward the Understanding Desert Center building fund which now stands at $292.86.

All Units of Understanding and other UFO clubs are invited to list their activities and lectures in the Bulletin Board. Just write them UP and send them in.

Excellent reports and reviews are still coming in concerning Hope Troxell's book "Wisdom of the Universe. We feel that this is one of the new books which you can't afford to miss. (*Understanding*, Volume 2 Number 9, September 1957)

Daniel Fry

If Daniel Fry published his magazine *Understanding* , Eugene Drake had his newsletter *Golden Light.* He advertised his books in "Understanding" Volume 2 Number 4, April 1957 in Books Recommended:

BOOKS RECOMMENDED

AS AN APPROACH TO UNDERSTANDING

ABOARD A FLYING SAUCER, by Truman Bethurum $3.00

OTHER TONGUES, OTHER FLESH, by Williamson 4.10

ARMY OF LIGHT, by Florence Donovan 1.50

I RODE A FLYING SAUCER, by George Van Tassel 1.00

AMERICA KNOW THY DESTINY, by Frank Spiva 2,50

UNITY IN THE SPIRIT, by Comtesse de Pierrefeu 2.50

INSIDE THE SPACE SHIPS, by George Adamski 3.50

INTO THIS WORLD AND OUT AGAIN, by George Van Tassel 1.50

MANY MANSIONS, by Gina Cerminara 3.75

PEACE, by Florence Donovan............. .50

SAUCER DIARY, by Israel Norkin 3.00

SECRET OF THE SAUCERS, by Orfeo Angelucci 3.00

STEPS TO THE STARS, by Daniel Fry (paper, $1.50) 2.50

THE VENUSIANS, by Lee Crandell...... 1.00

TO MEN OF EARTH, by Daniel Fry 1.00

UNIVERSE AND DR. EINSTEIN, by Lincoln Barnett ... 2.75

VISITORS FROM SPACE, by Eugene Drake 1.00

WHITE SANDS INCIDENT, by Daniel Fry 1.50

WISDOM IN PRACTICE, by Vera Stanley Alder............ .... 2.75

PUBLICATIONS

GOLDEN LIGHT .... Donatlon Basis

SAUCERS............... (four issues) $1.00

INTER-GALAXY NEWS .... .25

E. Nassau in his book entitled: *How to Combat Psychic Attack* (1957) refers to Eugene H. Drake as follows:

> The Fellowship of Golden Illumination (1014 So.Lake St., Los Angeles, Calif.). It is the focal point of concentrated rays from the Star Temple on the planet Venus, the Temple of Silence in the Himalayas, and Mount Shasta, California.

Director Eugene H. Drake says in this July 1956 issue of Golden Light that "a Desert Lodge has already been erected in the Upper Joshua Desert... We have had several contacts with space beings here." This desert region is about a hundred miles east of Los Angeles, California.

The Star Temple will be a healing center for the New Eras following the methods employed on the planet Venus with which Rev. Drake has been in contact for several years. He says: "One of the rooms will be dedicated to the arts... healing therapies using light, music, water, rejuvenation methods like the one used on the planet, Venus. The use of herbs, diets, oils, etc."

The temple will be in the shape of a five-pointed star, it must be constructed of glass and plastic in rainbow colors. It will have air conditioning, solar and indirect lighting. Four fountains will have colored lights playing through the spray. The health services will be carried out three times a day "with radiation cures that will be emitted every three hours."

We envy this wonderful man for the contact he has with the planet Venus, and we bless him for the good that he plans for all humanity by creating this Star Temple and spreading the healing rays from him to the whole world. However, this is only part of the great planned work. It will also have a classroom in which "instruction will be given in the different types of spiritual-magnetic-electrical and physical healing." There will also be a library, meditation, banquet and conference rooms, and of course, the usual service rooms. We wish The Fellowship of Golden Illumination every success now and in the years to come.

In the same area, seventeen miles north of Yucca Valley, is the College of Universal Wisdom, led by George Van Tassel.

In the paragraph mentioned above, it is found the idea for Van Tassel's Integratron. It seems that Van Tassel took the concept from Drake's Desert Lodge. The light, sound therapy rooms, and the rejuvenation method have the same concept as the Integratron. Also, it is essential to point out that both sites (Drake's Desert Lodge and Van Tassel's Integratron) were located very close to each other.

According to the swedish ufologist Håkan Blomqvist (2017), in 1949 or 1950, Drake published two small booklets. The first booklet was entitled: Visitors From Space. There is no publishing date printed but it must have been 1949 or early 1950. The second booklet, Life on the Planets. A Visit to Venus has 1950 as the publishing year. In one of the first pages of Visitors From Space there is a very interesting drawing of various types of "flying saucers". One of these craft is obviously the same type of bell shaped "venusian scout ship", with three spherical "landing gear" underneath, described and photographed by George Adamski. But Adamski never showed any photographs of this type of craft until 1952. And Drake's s booklet was published in 1949 or early 1950. So George Adamski was not the first to describe this bell shaped saucer. Did Adamski know of Eugene Drake and his booklet? [Taken Håkan Blomqvist

The United States of America,

To all whom these presents shall come, Greeting:

WHEREAS, a Certificate of the Land Office at **Los Angeles, California,** has been issued showing that full payment has been made by the claimant **Eugene Harry Drake,** pursuant to the provisions of the Act of Congress approved June 1, 1938 (52 Stat. 609), entitled "An Act to provide for the purchase of public lands for home and other sites," and the acts supplemental thereto, for the following-described land:

San Bernardino Meridian, California.

T. 3 N., R. 4 E.,

Sec. 15, E½NW¼SW¼NW¼.

The area described contains **5.00** acres, according to the Official Plat of the Survey of the said Land, on file in the Bureau of Land Management:

NOW KNOW YE, That the UNITED STATES OF AMERICA, in consideration of the premises, and in conformity with the several Acts of Congress in such case made and provided, HAS GIVEN AND GRANTED, and by these presents DOES GIVE AND GRANT unto the said claimant and to the heirs of the said claimant the Tract above described; TO HAVE AND TO HOLD the same, together with all the rights, privileges, immunities, and appurtenances, of whatsoever nature, thereunto belonging, unto the said claimant and to the heirs and assigns of the said claimant forever; subject to any vested and accrued water rights for mining, agricultural, manufacturing, or other purposes, and rights to ditches and reservoirs used in connection with such water rights, as may be recognized and acknowledged by the local customs, laws, and decisions of courts; and there is reserved from the lands hereby granted, a right-of-way thereon for ditches or canals constructed by the authority of the United States. Excepting and reserving, also, to the United States, all coal, oil, gas, and other mineral deposits, in the land so patented, together with the right to prospect for, mine, and remove the same according to the provisions of said Act of June 1, 1938. This patent is subject to a right-of-way not exceeding **33** feet in width, for roadway and public utilities purposes, to be located **along the boundaries of said land.**

IN TESTIMONY WHEREOF, the undersigned authorized officer of the Bureau of Land Management, in accordance with the provisions of the Act of June 17, 1948 (62 Stat., 476), has, in the name of the United States, caused these letters to be made Patent, and the Seal of the Bureau to be hereunto affixed.

GIVEN under my hand, in the District of Columbia, the **ELEVENTH** day of **DECEMBER** in the year of our Lord one thousand nine hundred and **FIFTY-SIX** and of the Independence of the United States the one hundred and **EIGHTY-FIRST.**

[SEAL]

For the Director, Bureau of Land Management.

By _Rose M. Beall_
_____
Chief, Patents Section.

Patent Number **1167115**

Certificate of Land Office issued to Eugene Harry Drake in 1956 for a 5-acre plot of land in San Bernardino, California

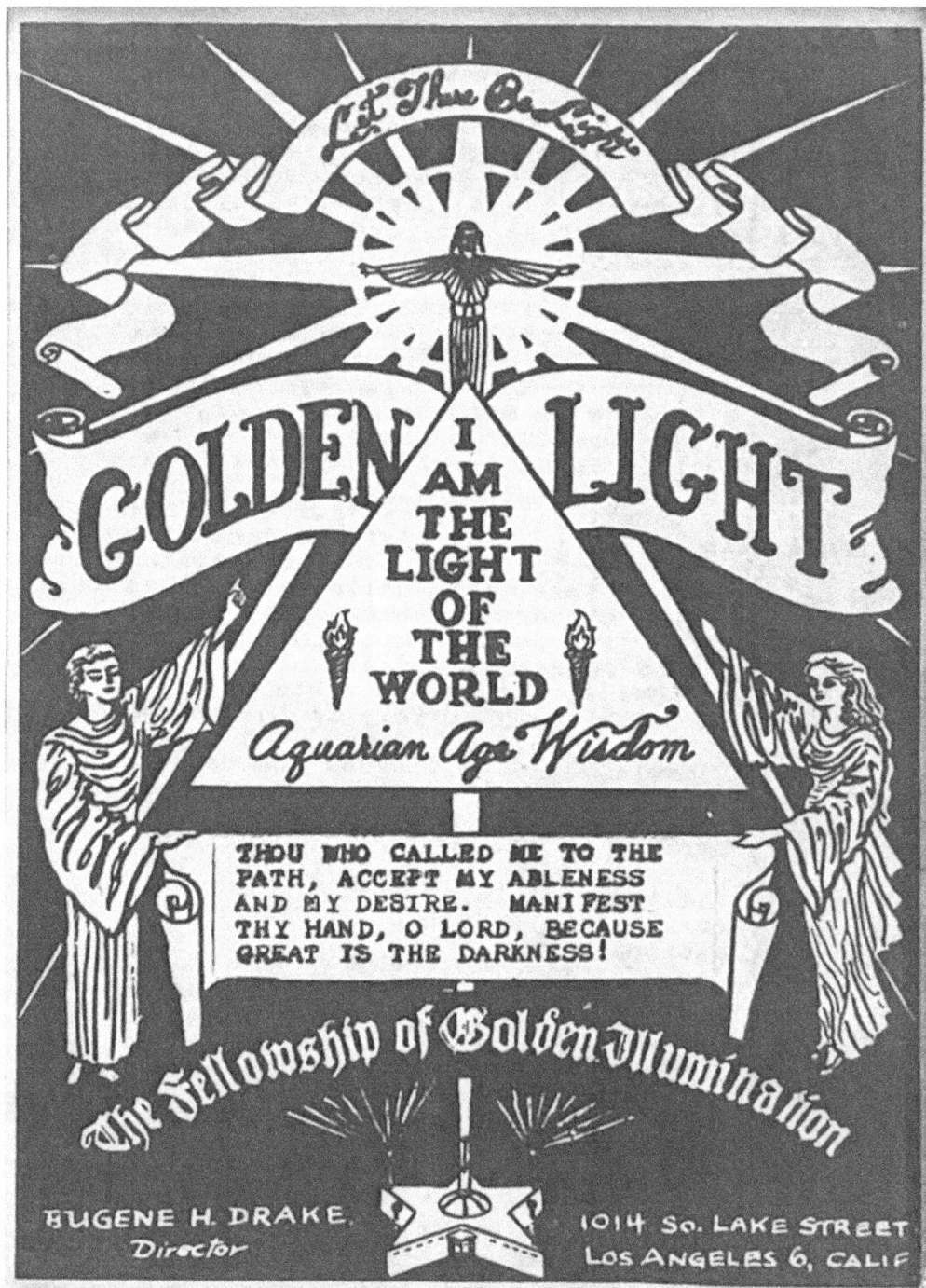

Golden Light; The Fellowship of Golden Illumination. No date (c. 1958). 8 pp. in purple pictorial stapled wraps, 5.5 x 8.5 message pamphet from Drake about the Fellowship proposing a Spiritual Center and Retreat, The Star Temple, which is to be constructed of glass and plastics of rainbow colors .This Star Temple will be the focal point for concentrated rays from the Star Temple on the Planet Venus, The Temple of Silence in Himalayas, and from Mt. Shasta, California. Includes a space to fill out a donation or pledge to the Star Temple Building Fund. Drake, who claimed contact with aliens, also published two pamphlets in the late 1950s: Visitors from Space and Life on the Planets: A Visit to Venus.

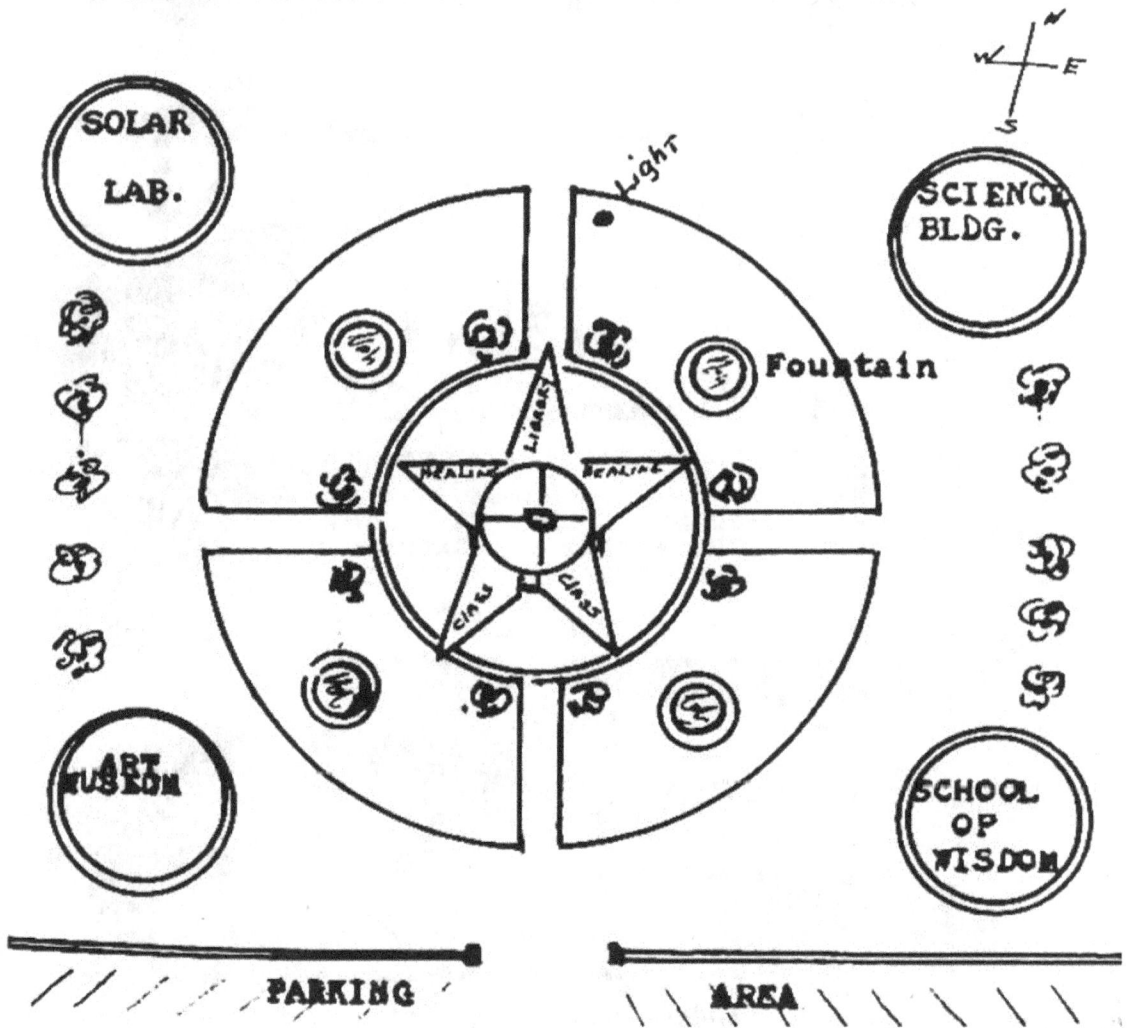

Top view of Drake's Spiritual Center and Retreat. No date (c. 1958)

VISITORS FROM
SPACE
The Fellowship of Golden Illumination
EUGENE H. DRAKE, Director
1014 So. LAKE STREET · LOS ANGELES 6, CALIF.

Drake H. Eugene, *Visitors from Space: Space Ships, Discs, Flying Saucers.* The Fellowship of GoldenIllumination, 1014 South Lake Street, Los Angeles, California, 1949-50. 38 p.

FLYING SAUCERS

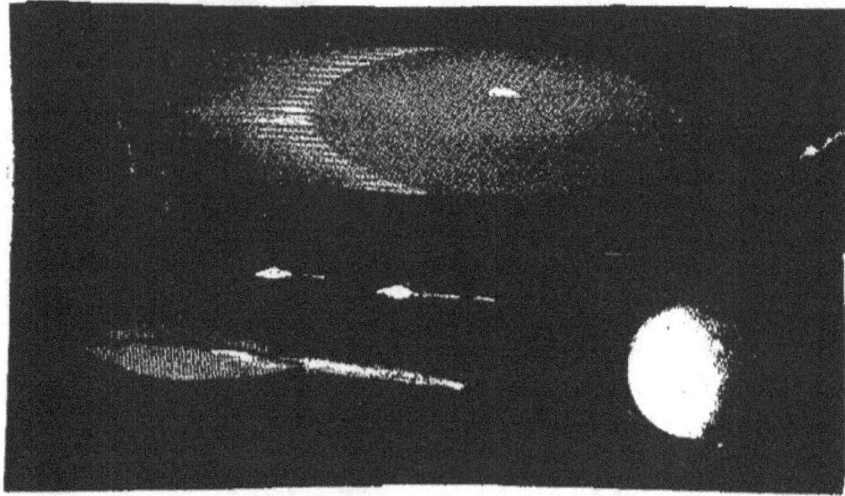

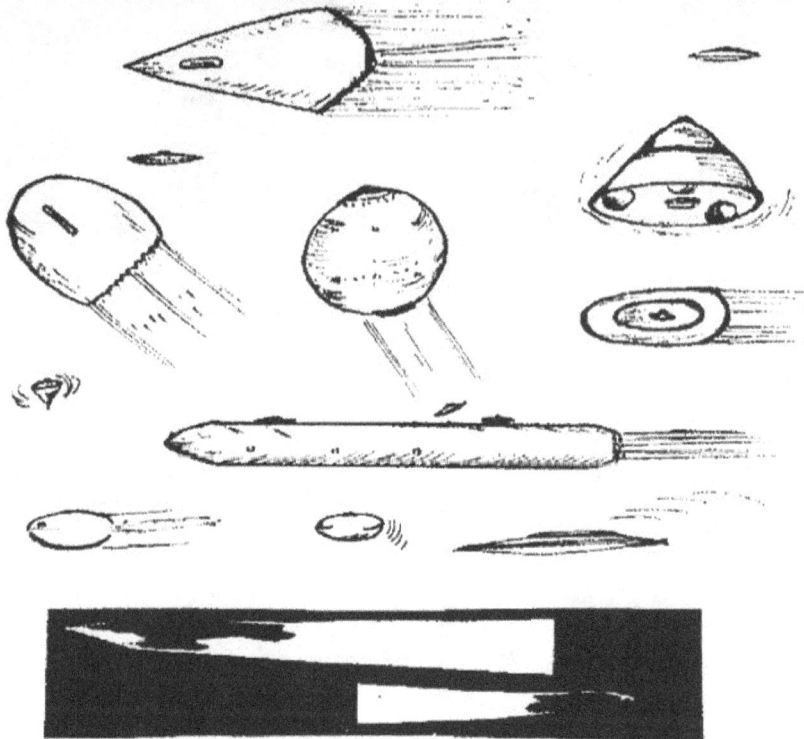

Page 2 from Drake H. Eugene, *Visitors from Space: Space Ships, Discs, Flying Saucers.* The Fellowship of Golden Illumination, 1014 South Lake Street, Los Angeles, California, 1949-50. 38 p.

Adamski like Drake's Flying Saucer. Takenfrom page 2 in: Drake H. Eugene, *Visitors from Space: Space Ships, Discs, Flying Saucers.* **The Fellowship of GoldenIllumination, 1014 South Lake Street, Los Angeles, California, 1949-50. 38 p.**

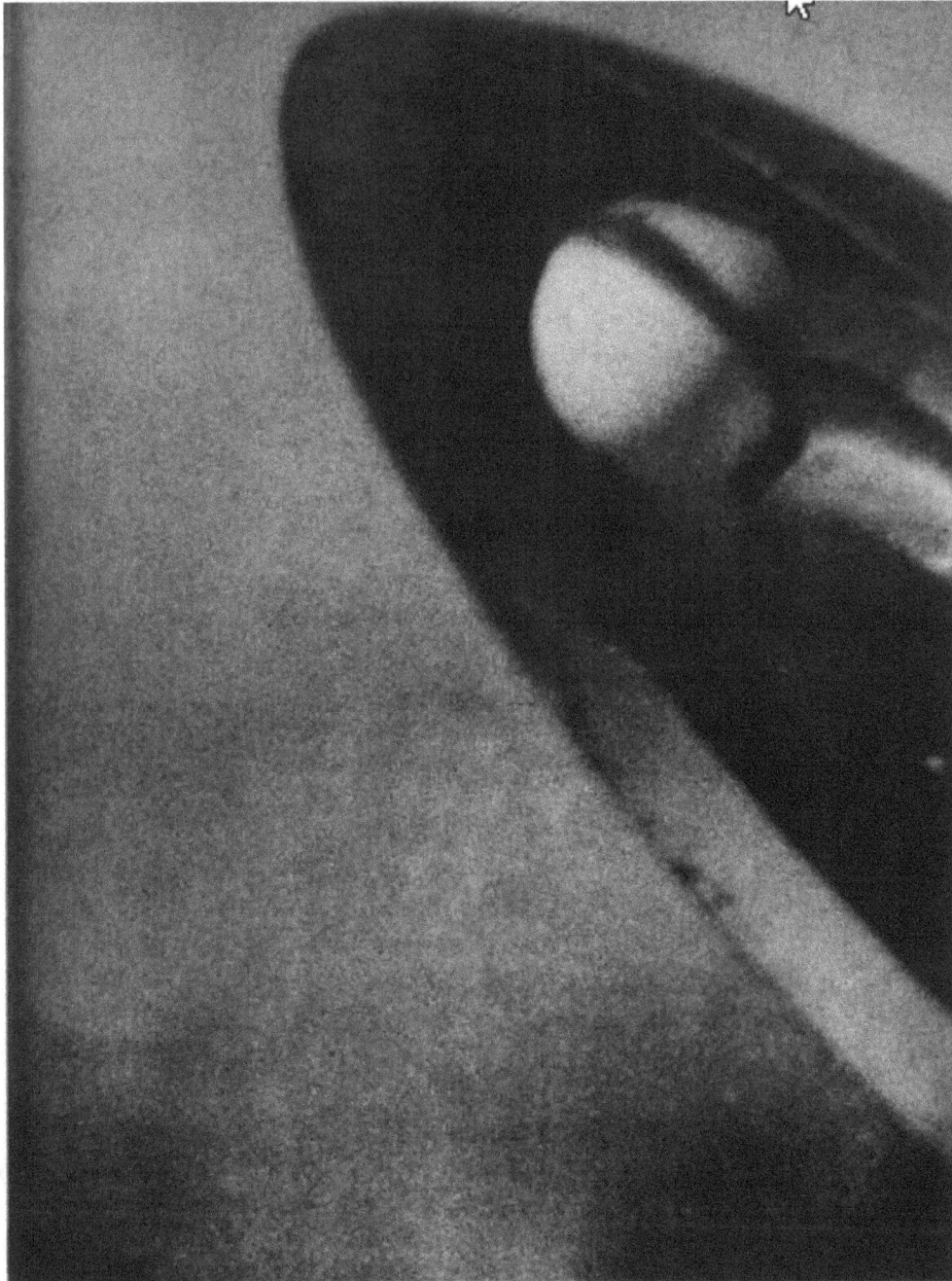

5 DETAIL OF LANDING GEAR

This, the third of the telescopic series of pictures made on 13 December 1952, gives a detailed view of one of the three landing spheres by means of which the saucer can apparently land in any direction. This simple ingenious arrangement would also facilitate manhandling on the ground or in the stowage decks of great carrier ships.

Taken from *Flying saucers have landed* (1953) by Leslie, Desmond, and Adamski, George

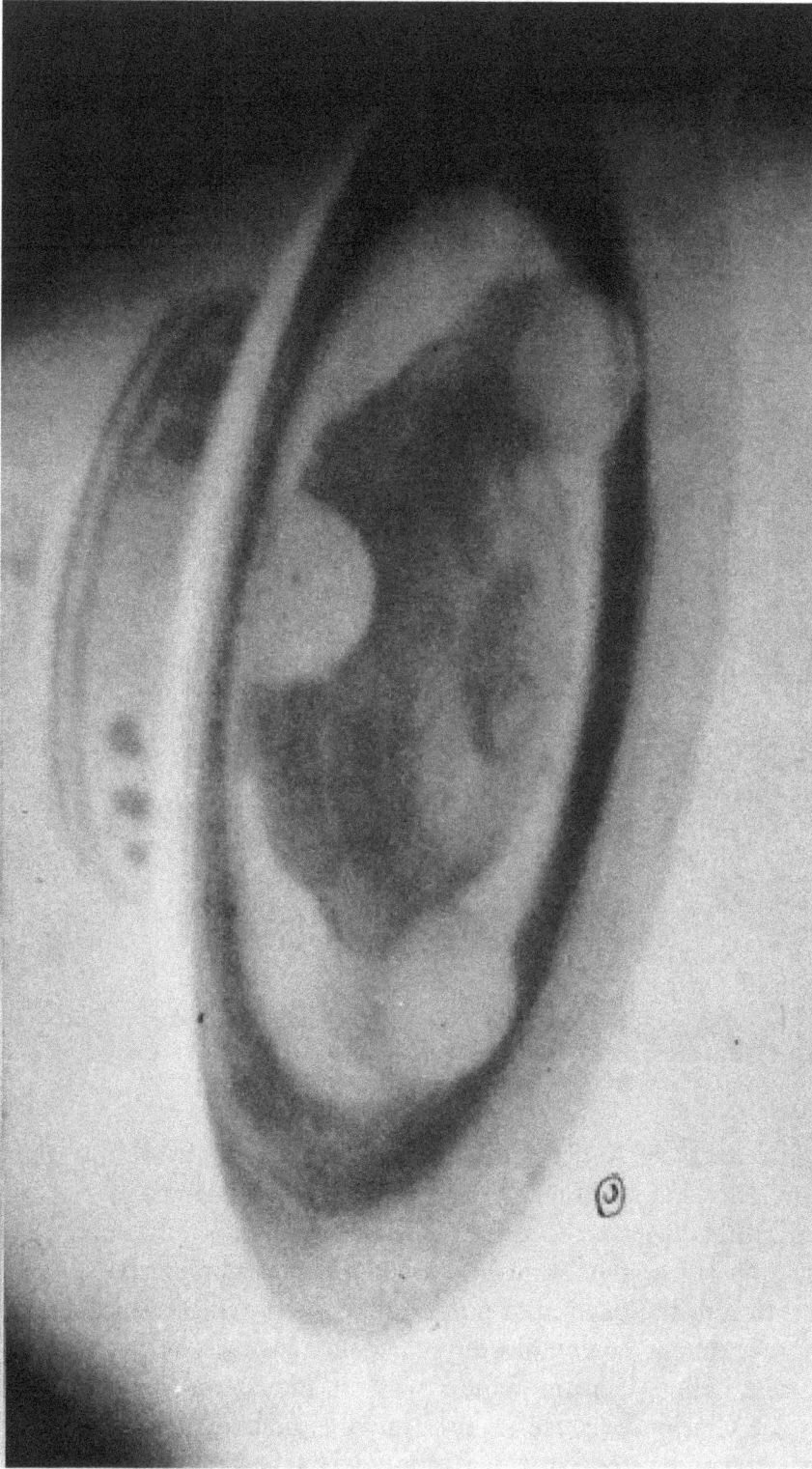

Taken from *Flying saucers have landed* (1953) by Leslie, Desmond,, and Adamski, George,

´s blog: The UFO contactee no one investigated. On Line [2021]:https://ufoarchives.blogspot.com/2017/01/the-ufo-contactee-no-one-investigated.html]

Another contactee that is deeply in debt with Drake is Truman Bethurum. Before Bethurum, Drake claimed to have been visited by two Venusian flying saucer pilots named Aramian and Estralon. However, Drake's contact was in 1950, while Bethurum's supposedly occurred in 1952-1953.

George Van Tassel's Integratron

During this time, Bethurum was 55 and beside working in an asphalt mixing plant, he had a part time job as a fortune teller and spiritual advisor. According to Bethurum, one night eight to ten little men awakened him as he was sleeping near his "rig," and he noticed a flying saucer near them on the ground. The little men took the curious Bethurum aboard the "scow," as they called it, and introduced him to the captain, a gorgeous woman named Aura Rhanes. She was similar to Earth women except for her extraordinary beauty. Aura explained that she and her crew came from a planet called Clarion which was in the same solar system as Earth. Astronomers could not see Clarion because its orbit always placed it directly behind the sun. The Clarionites had been coming to Earth for many years and were able to walk around unnoticed. They were "very religious, understanding, kind, friendly and . . . trusting." They had come to Earth, Aura explained, to reaffirm the values of marriage, family, and fidelity, because a "dreadful Paganism" was at work and the Clarionites did not want to see Earth people destroy themselves. Aura feared atomic war and wanted to prevent Earth from blowing itself up, an event that would perpetrate "considerable confusion" in space. In the course of their lengthy discussions, Aura explained to Bethurum in detail the idyllic quality of life on Clarion, a life that Earth people could enjoy if they thought and behaved correctly. Before the Clarionites departed for home, Bethurum met with them eleven times. Sometimes he saw them in cafes, but there they ignored him because they did not want to reveal their identities. When they finally left and Bethurum told his story, no one believed him except George Adamski, who encouraged him to publicize his experiences. Bethurum thought Adamski was a great man and an authority on space travel.

Buck Nelson (left) and Truman Bethurum (right)

Fantasy created a false world around a person's love, but this has its limits. In this case, the limit is that the object of affection does not exist. Bethurum had the inability to stop thinking about Aura Rhanes, becoming a sexual obsession with her image. It's important to keep in mind that sexual obsessions are not the same thing as sexual fantasies. Whereas sexual fantasies are typically related to pleasure or desire, attainable or not, sexual obsessions are unwanted and distressing thoughts associated with anxiety, shame, or self-loathing. This obsession is projected in his description of this imaginary woman (Rhanes).

Bethurum was not the only one to claim contact with Rhanes. The New Jersey ham operator

Dominick Lucchesi claimed to have received a strange invitation over his radio set on a restricted frequency and then has a rendezvous with the beautiful space commander Aura Rhanes, disembarking from a flying saucer in a remote corner of New Jersey countryside. Lucchesi sketched his version of Commander Aura Rhanes based on his encounter with her ,and the description provided him by California contactee Truman Bethurum.

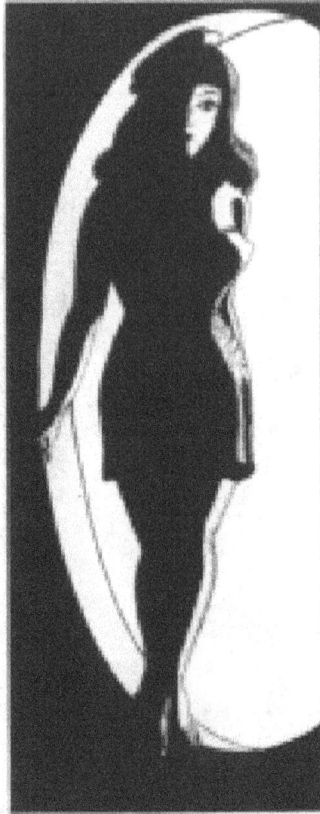

**Taken from the Gray Barker UFO Collection, Clarksburg-Harrison Public Library .
Clarksburg, West Virginia.**

The accounts of Adamski and other self-described alien contactees, such as Truman Bethurum (*Aboard a flying saucer,* 1954), Donald Fry (*The White Sands Incident,* 1954), Orfeo Angelucci (*The Secret of the Saucers,* 1955, and Howard Menger (*From Outer Space to You*, 1959) stories contained recurrent situations. It seems that it was a common practice that male contactees met with their beautiful human extraterrestrial counterparts. Another contactee who met a beautiful spacewoman was Orfeo Angelucci. After an initial meeting in May of 1952, he spent seven days with the extraterrestrials in January of 1953. Unfortunately, he remembered little of his experience until something triggered his memory in September of that year. In 1955 he published his story as *The Secret of the Saucers,* an account rich with emotional detail about the beauty of his space-traveling friends and their peace-loving way of life. Although the space beings said, they had an ancient kinship with humanity. Earth itself, they said, had become a purgatory because of human hate, selfishness, and cruelty. The aliens commissioned Angelucci to take their message of love and peace to the entire world.

George Adamski calling Et's at the Giant Rock Interplanetary Spacecraft Convention. May, 1957

Similarly, contactee Howard Menger appeared in the public eye in 1956 to say that he had had contacts with extraterrestrial entities since childhood. When he was ten, he met a beautiful blonde spacewoman who told him that her people were contacting "their own" and that they were trying to help humanity solve its problems. When Menger was twenty-four he claimed that he saw this same apparently ageless woman emerged from a landed saucer. Sometime after he entered into the public spotlight, Menger met an attractive young blonde (terrestrial) woman whom he said he immediately recognized as the sister of the spacewoman he had seen twice before. He divorced his current wife and married the "'sister," whom he later realized had been his Venusian lover in a previous life when he had been a Saturnian.

Also, there is necessary to mention the real babe Dolores Barrios, who was from Venus, according to some believers. During the Summer of 1954 (August 7- August 8), the first UFO Congress was held at Mt. Palomar in San Diego, California. The main event was the panels of three contactees, George Adamski, Daniel Fry, and Truman Bethurum about their alien encounters. George Adamski claimed he met friendly Nordic-like aliens, whom he called "Space Brothers". These Space Brothers were from Venus and landed their flying saucer in the Colorado desert by November 20, 1952. In his contact with the Venusians, he had the opportunity to fly in their craft. During Adamski's presentation, he explained the Venusians' intentions and morphological structure, just like human beings, with various minor aspects. Their appearance was almost undetected, and they could live among us unnoticed. To illustrate it, Adamski presented a painting of a Venusian he called Orthon. By the end of the first day, just a few hours after Adamski's presentation, the audience noticed the presence of three individuals similar to those described by Adamski. The rumor started that Venusians were among them, two men and a woman. Their features resembled the description presented hours before by Adamski, as the type of extraterrestrial that came from Venus and walked on planet Earth. The rumor in the crowd spread that they were the "Venusians" in disguise. It is the general belief that these three "Venusians" were: Dolores Barrios, a fashion designer from New York, and her two friends: Donald Morand and Bill Jackmart, from Manhattan Beach, California. Barrios had a protruding bone structure in the middle of the forehead, extending to the nasal form, and deep eyes with large eyelashes.

However, Barrios attended the Van Tassel's 1954 Giant Rock UFO Convention in Landers, California. News reporter Don Dwiggins interviewed her. He concluded in his article that Barrios was not from Venus, instead, she was from Venice, California.

DOLORES BARRIOS
From Venus or Venice?

Mistery In The Sky! Saucer Meets Baffled
<u>Daily News</u> **(Los Angeles, California)**
05 Apr 1954, Mon. Page 3, 33

Drake described his Venusian beauty Aramia as:

The Commander of one of these Space Ships, known as Aramia, is 5 feet 10 inches tall. Very dignified. Solidly built, fairly broad through the shoulders. His hair is long and golden. The cheeks are pink, eyes large and blue, his chin strong. He has a very pleasing expression. He wearB a tight fitting tunic of pearl shade silk, with gold and blue trim, the collar of which is three inches high,-open a little at the throat, with gold tabs at the ends. On the shoulders of the tunic are golden epaulets--somewhat simlliar to the "boards'* worn by naval officers. He wears tight fitting trunks of same material, pearl silk, with a golden zipper up one side of the calf. His shoes are a soft golden metallic material. While his manner is gracious it is very commanding. One can feel the magnetic force emanating from his person. His command ship is from the Planet Venus.

ARAMIA   Estralon

"The Cage" is the first pilot episode of the American television series *Star Trek*. It was completed on January 22, 1965. The episode was written by Gene Roddenberry and directed by Robert Butler. The year is 2254 and the USS Enterprise, under the command of Captain Christopher Pike, receives a radio distress call from the fourth planet in the Talos star group. A landing party is assembled and beamed down to investigate. Tracking the distress signal to its source, the landing party discovers a camp of survivors from a scientific expedition missing for eighteen years. Amongst the survivors is a beautiful young woman named Vina. Captivated by her beauty, Pike is caught off guard and is captured by the Talosians, a race of humanoids with bulbous heads who live beneath the planet's surface. It is revealed that the distress call, and the crash survivors, except for Vina, are just illusions created by the Talosians to lure the Enterprise to the planet. While imprisoned, Pike uncovers the Talosians' plans to repopulate their ravaged world using him and Vina as breeding stock for a race of slaves.

The Talosians use their power to make Pike experience illusions in different testing scenarios based on his memories to interest him in Vina. Vina appeared as a beautiful woman in various settings. First as a Rigellian princess, then as a damsel in distress in a crumbling castle confronted by a giant alien warrior, then as a loving, compassionate farm girl, and finally as a seductive green-skinned Orion babe. Pike resists all forms. After an earlier landing party failed to gain entry from the surface into the talosian compound, six members of the Enterprise crew prepare to beam into the Talosians underground complex, but only Pike's first officer (Majel Barrett) and yeoman (Laurel Goodwin)—both women—materialize in Pike's cell to offer further temptation.

Susan Oliver on *Star Trek* "The Cage" as an Orion slave girl

The Vina Syndrome is a kind of obsessive love disorder" (OLD) in which the contactee becomes obsessed with an imaginary female gorge extraterrestrial woman. It is an illusion, a fantasy, a mirage born out of the contactees' unhappiness with his private life. It is a coping mechanism to fulfill the contactees' need for love and to be loved. It is the psychological need to create a Vina-like character like in the *Star Trek* pilot episode.

Most of these contactees postulate a series of close encounters with alien visitations that are a kind of "angelnauts". Borrowing from its ufological origins, the theology assumes that extraterrestrials are interested in assisting human beings to spiritual self-improvement, self-transformation, and technological development to higher levels. A cult leader, acting as a "prophet" who has the gift of communicating with the angelnauts, who thinks that he has been misinterpreted during his lifetime due to his advanced ways of thinking about society, he is the key figure in these cults. In essence, these contactee prophets are like Jesus Christ that was misunderstood, rejected and not received by the world. The "prophet" is the "chosen one" by the angelnauts to receive the E.T revelations for his/her (mostly his) extraordinary gift and advance spiritual development. These prophets had acquired knowledge "beyond our understanding". They claim that the world would experience a "great spiritual awakening" with the arrival of the angelnauts, and human society will never move forward as long as the "angelnauts" do not cooperate with earthlings. The prophecized a new age of enlightenment humans with greater intelligence created with the help of angelnauts. The imaginary female gorge extraterrestrial woman described by Drake, Bethurum, and others are these "angelnauts".

The similarities in Drake's work with the contactees who followed him are undeniable. Drakes has his Fellowship of *Golden Illumination*, and the contactees that came after him developed similar saucerian organizations like: George Van Tassel and his *College of Universal Wisdom,* George Adamsky and his *Royal Order of Tibet*, George King and his *Aetherius Society.* Also, the founder of *Scientology* and *Dianetics*, L. Ron Hubbard, an SCI-FI writer, and Frank E. Stranges, a reverend.

He died on February 21, 1973 in Los Angeles. He was 82.

Some of the information and message presented in the two of Drake's booklets appear sincere and genuine in feelings. But whatever was the metaphysical meaning of his writings; Drake was a crucial figure in UFO history. George Adamski after him, and the other contactees that followed him, are much in debt with Drake's idea. It seems that they almost copied from Drake's booklets. Historians, sociologists, and ufologists, in general, could find many fascinating clues about the origin of the UFO movement by studying Eugene Harry Drake.

Editor
Saucerian Publisher, 2022

F O R E W A R D

The data compiled herein is presented to those interested in the subject of
visitations from space by beings of superior intelligence with the hope that they
be alerted to the fast changing conditions
as they affect this planet.

Even tho the atomic warfare never
takes place, the fact that several nations
are firing such test bombs of destructive
magnitude, is creating great mental harm
with individuals as well as monstrosities
of diabolical activity that will come into manifestation at a later period and in
this respect alone warrants cessation.

Vibratory waves are penetrating into
gas belts in the crust of the earth which
are bringing increased earthquake disturb-
ances; effecting the atmosphere causing a
repetition of storms and floods, the melting of the polar caps, but worse of all is
the hate pattern being built up in the consciousness of peoples the world over.

Creative law is being violated by
this activity, threatening humanity every
where.

Black Magicians can do nothing but
destroy. They do not know how to build,
only to tear down.   Psychotic minds are
unconsciously alined with them.

The Elder Brothers from Space, the
forces of the White Brotherhood are here
in greater array than any time since man
walked the earth. They have the answers.

We salute them.

FLYING SAUCERS

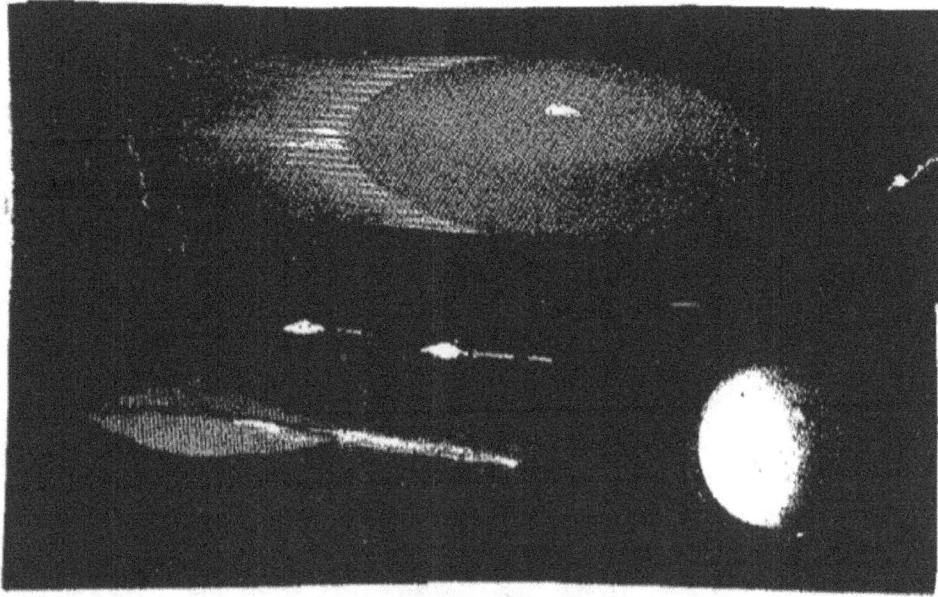

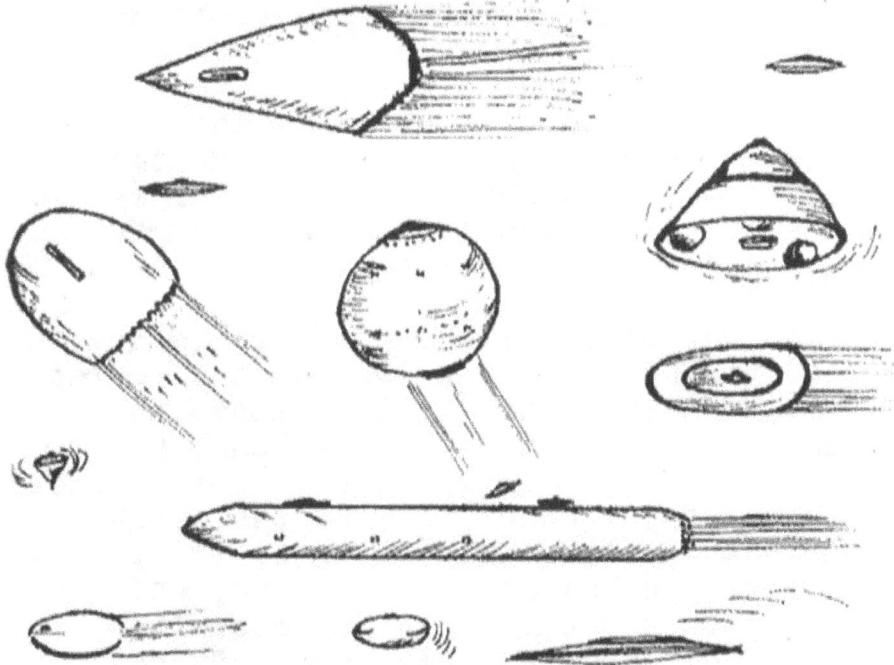

VISITORS FROM SPACE

SPACE SHIPS -DISCS- FLYING SAUCERS

BY
Eugene H. Drake,
Los Angeles, Cal.

........oOo.........

For a long time space craft have had
this planet under observation. We have
been in contact with them since 1930. At
that time we were in Santa Monica, and
contact was made in a large field where
the Santa Monica City College is now located. Only during the past few years
have they chosen to reveal their presence.

These space ships, with their discs
or flying saucers, as some call them, had
their commanders so desired, could have
and still can, take over this planet at
any time. However, they have no desire
to interfere with our life here. They
only wish to assist us in arriving at a
clearer understanding of the immutable
laws governing this and all solar systems
and to help us build a more wonderful,
beautiful and peaceful civilization.

Some of these space ships are huge in
length and diameter. One of the parent
ships in the upper regions above this planet is at least 7000 feet long, 500 feet
in diameter, with a crew of approximately
2500 beings, consisting of the officers
in charge, with pilots, navigators, obs-
ervers, technicans, scientists, and other members required in the operation of
this ship and many smaller craft being
used in their visitation plan.

These ships with their intricate mechanism are powered by a form of electro-
magnetic force. They are heavily armed

with powerful ray weapons. They can operate
at tremenduous speeds. They cruise about
27,000 miles per hour, our timing. Although
when traveling through outer space from one
planet to another, they use speeds far in ex-
cess of this. They do not carry fuel such
as our planes use but are able to convert energy of light into electro-magnetic force,to
propel their craft. Through the use of ray
machines they can erect a vacuum-like condition above and around their craft to enable
them to move up or down, sideways or reverse
their direction, or hover visible or invisible; to convert their craft into a fluid like state, beaming it to where they want to
go in a very short period.

They come into our atmospheric belts from
their planets not in solid form but in an etheric form. Upon entering our atmosphere
they, through their superior knowledge, change the atomic elements in the construction
of these ships and materialize them into the
density which they are now using. The beings
on these various craft are also passed from
the etheric to a dense form of matter and appear to materialize. By speeding up the vibratory frequency of the atoms of the elements
of which these craft are made, as stated before, they can move with great speeds invisible to our physical sight, and when they
desired slow them down and congeal this atomic energy to a more solid form. There are
elements known to them of which our scient -
ists have no knowledge or understanding, which they use and mold in whatever form, idea
or shape they wish.

The fact that we of earth have been expl-
oding atomic bombs, and plan to use them with hydrogen or cobalt bombs in warfare, is
one of the reasons why these space visitors
have come into our density. For these vibratory waves have disturbed the etheric atmosphere around this planet, punching holes

as it were in the same, and these waves have
penetrated lines of magnetic force and spir-
aled up to other planets of our solar system.
They have also disturbed the etheric subst -
ance in what we call the lower and upper heavens around the earth and the etheric beings
occupying these realms or worlds, which are
as dense to them as our cities are to us.
Many of these inhabitants have been moved to
portions of the stratosphere where explosions
do not disturb them.

Therefore, these space craft were sent to
investigate such activity. Anything distur-
ing the etheric atmospheric belts around this
planet also effect the other planets of the
solar system; each being part of the whole.

The Commander in charge of this expedit -
ion to whom I have been talking, advised that
any wide scale atomic or hydrogen bombings
will necessitate the use of powers beyond our
conception to eliminate laboratories, airpl-
ane plants, planes, and such plants where
such bombs are made and assembled, and the
planes carrying them, as well as take in charge the beings controlling such destructive
activity.

Many of these space visitors are from Venus, Mars, Saturn, Jupiter and Uranus, altho
some of them are coming now from other solar
systems, working in harmony with those whom
we call Elder Brothers of this solar system.

This solar system is in charge of a Great
Cosmic Being who directs all life under the
Great Creative Plan. The Elder Brothers or
Etherians work under His direct supervision.

Civilization will not be permitted to be
destroyed as it was almost during the struggle between the Titans and the Atlans, LaMu-
rians prior to the sinking of Lemuria and
Atlantis.

Should they land in our midst we would
quickly realize how inferior we are, how much
we must learn of life, brotherly love, of which we talk a great deal but practice little,
and of the laws governing creation.

An increasing number of space craft have
assembled in the upper regions over this planet. The beings on them number more than two
and one-half millions, with millions more on
the way.   They are assembling for the increased violence on the earth, the speeding up
of the so-called cold war, and also to keep
the atmosphere cleared of radio-active vibrations.   Not that they are particularly interested in saving us from our own created
destructive activity, but to preserve the
earth itself, of which they are the guardi-
ans, and to establish a new civilization as
needful during every New Age.

They have the situation now under their
control.   They have plugged up the holes in
our atmosphere.   They have sent what we call
fire-balls blazing thru our air to purify the
same of radio-active particles and to prevent
further vibratory waves traveling to the other planets.   Rather confining the same to the
where they are originating.

There are a great many different types and
classes of Space Craft in the fleets above the
earth.   We would say over 250 kinds. The Fleet
Commanders use ships of the 7000 foot length
class.   Sub-Commanders those of about 5000 ft.
long.   All of them heavily armed and protected
against attack.   As stated before, they are
manned by beings from the planets mentioned.
The far side of the earth's moon, the side not
seen by people of earth or by astronomers, is
often used as an assembling point.

The Space Craft are mostly cigar-shape

and reflect a silvery-golden color. Some of
the discs are flat, some global, reflecting
a silvery light. The energy which surrounds
these craft when in motion gives forth such
colors as blue, green, reddish blue, orange
and lavender.

The escort and fighter type craft are several hundred feet long. Some 100 feet, 25
to 15 feet in diameter. They carry from 20
to 50 in their crews, are driven by cosmic
energy, converted into electro-magnetic power.

Another type of craft resembles a dough-
nut, carry a crew of about 50. These are
used as laboratories. They are circular ,
125 feet across, about 25 feet thick. Here
all data is checked, analyzed, and transmi-
ted to other craft. Atmospheric conditions
are scientifically studied. All magnetic
vortexes charted.

Another type is 100 feet across, circular, 25 feet thick, capable of carrying about 20 each.

The global type have several levels or
decks. These are also observational ships,
electro-magnetically driven.

Smaller disc shaped craft range from 50
feet across down to 15 feet. Some are 15
feet thick, others only 7 feet. They carry
crews from 8 to 2 persons. These are some
of the craft that come close to the earth
checking on all plane plants, landing fields,
laboratories, plants where bomb parts are
made and assembled, and also where mining
operations for uranium are conducted.

Another type, controlled by larger craft
range from 15 feet across to others only 6
feet. Others only two feet across, shaped

like tops. Some of these smaller craft have
been mistaken for fire-balls. These top-
like objects are made of an electronic substance whirling at such speeds they seem tra-
nsparent. These are used for photographic
purposes by which the inside as well as the
outside of any object or substance is photographed. These are controlled by magnetic
beams similiar to our radar. Such pictures
taken are viewed on board the space ships on
what we would call space mirrors or screens,
but theirs are vastly superior to anything we
have constructed.

They have a visa-scope which they can fo-
cus so minutely as to look not only into a
room where people are but right into their
brains, watching the pulsations when they
are talking or thinking. The brain cells
throw off colorful lights as they vibrate.
Some vibrate but little. The right side of
many earth people brains are almost in a do-
rmant state.

They have an instrument that is about a
foot square on the top, and then is bell shaped (somewhat like a green pepper), flat on
the bottom, which they set in the middle of
a craft, and from the light energy picked up
from our atmosphere by this instrument it be -
gins to oscillate. The top section moving
clock-wise. The other parts of the bell portion moving both counter clock-wise and clock-wise. As this movement increases in tempo
waves of light energy are pushed out in the
ship and beyond its walls for considerable
distance and these waves are of many colors.
This motion vibrates so fast that the craft
sets up a slight humming sound, and under
control of the operator shoots out into space
at terrific speeds. This is the color seen
by earth people as the craft travels through
our atmosphere.

We have called these smaller craft and

discs by many names, such a flying saucers,
"fire-balls", "foo-balls", or vortexes of
electro-magnetic energy. Some such conditions do exist in our atmosphere, but they
should not be confused with any of the craft referred to herein.

Every part of the earth's surface where
destructive war activity is centered has
been viewed, all air-fields and plants charted, also all laboratories. All areas
where uranium and other minerals are being
mined for use in the manufacture of atomic
or hydrogen bombs listed. All world leaders are under their surveillance. All so-
called secret meetings, plans, operations,
designs are known to these space beings.
Invisible watchers are in the midst of all
meetings, noting, recording and photograph-
ing all that takes place that has destruction in mind. Through the use of the visa-
scope they can check on every phase of our
life.

As the mission of these craft is a help-
ful and peaceful one, no harm is intended
to any earth beings unless a hostile move
is made against them. They are now in contact with certain individuals who have tak-
en up physical embodiment on earth to work
with these space beings in the unfolding of
the New Age Plan, to assist in the building
of a better civilization.

Should any hostile action be taken against them they will quickly remove the same.
By using certain cosmic forces which they
are thoroly familiar with they would easily
disintegrate any such hostile craft before
it or any of its guided missles are disch-
arged. Airplanes would also be prevented
from leaving the ground for such an attack.
Pilots and operators could be placed in an
unconscious or sleep state unable to perform

any functions, and forts, plants or operat-
ional points disintegrated through demagnet-
ization. Hostile planes could be enveloped
in a field of force that would suspend them
helplessly in the air. They would also quickly take in charge and using such powers unknown to us of earth, pick up the leaders directing such hostile actions against them
into the 4th, 5th, 6th, and higher dimensi-
ons, into the presence of the Space Beings.
People would say they must have disappeared
in a blaze of high vibratory light.   They
would make their own ships invisible traveling in the midst of the hostile planes without being detected. This information should
serve to convince earthlings how futile these
efforts would be against beings of such superior intelligence. It would be wise   for
earth leaders and people to concentrate on
ways of peace and brotherly love rather on
war and destruction.

Many of these smaller craft will be seen
in the near future, during the period of great stress coming upon the earth. Some of
the larger space ships may be seen also. Their appearance will serve to awake millions
that there are beings of far superior intelligence to earth people on other planets.

When the new races are established in North and South America, in Africa, Australia
and New Zealand, people of earth will have
the actual experience and opportunity of seeing some of these Beings in dense forms; learn of their great wisdom and power.

If we would realize that our astronomers
have photographed solar systems and galaxies
with millions of planets, millions of light
years from the earth, we must accept the fact
that intelligent beings are dwelling and act-
ively engaged in their form of life expression on a great number of planets. They are
occupied by beings whose atomic cell and or-
ganic structures are somewhat different from

ours, in which they are able to function in their atmospheric conditions just as we do in the earth, and from what we are told could learn a great deal.

Many of our scientists, musicians, poets, etc., have received much of their understanding from higher minds both carnate and disincarnate who have drawn close and impressed upon their consciousness ideas which they claim as their own. This intelligence originated in the higher spheres of consciousness and was given to them that humanity be benefited and civilizations lifted to more wonderful expression. Many wonderful inventions have been seized by unscrupulous people, capitalized upon for their own personal gain with little real thought for the upliftment of humanity, except they had the financial means to purchase the same.

Many visitations have been made to the earth since its formation and cooling by these Elder Brothers of Space, and during periods of wars and great tribulation. This is not the first time that the earth has been at the doorway of a great Golden Age. In the history of earth's civilizations there have been several. Five times the earth has stood in the path of destruction, and several times it has been thrown out of its original orbit. It is not now in the orbit it began its first movement in space.

This is the end of a great cosmic cycle of 2-1/2 million years, as well as an age cycle, and a period cycle, so drastic changes are due to change the inhabitants of the earth as well as the earth's land areas, as well as its position in the heavens.

Our heaven and earth are being moved along with the other planets of our solar system through space at a tremenduous speed

into another part of the great universe, into the auric field of a Central Sun, invisible now to our astronomical instruments.
This will alter the face of the earth bringing up now sunken bodies of land, like the
old Murian continent, until the water area of
the earth is greatly reduced. The atmosphere around the earth, the lower heavens, is
now undergoing and will continue to undergo
changes until a new heavens or atmosphere
surrounds it, vibrating at a higher more refined degree.

These flying discs or saucers have been
seen in most every country on the planet.
Many hundreds of such observations have been
noted in the past few years. Many were not
seen at all. Many pages of these sightings
could be filled--made by reputable individuals. Many were seen in the daylight which
refuted the idea of falling stars, fire-balls,
etc. Many were seen fairly close up. Some
pictures have been taken of them showing a
density like our own planes.

They have been sighted in many states of the
nation. In Canada, many countries of South
America, Korea, New Zealand, Australia, Ita-
ly, France, Germany, Russia, Sweden, Norway,
England, Spain, Siberia, Japan, and several
places in Africa, over uranium mines, and elsewhere.

Almost a century ago a phenomena of lights
were seen in England and became known as the
Durham Lights.

The newspapers were filled with stories of
mysterious cigar-shaped airships in 1897
seen in various parts of the country. It was
reported that the lights and men on board
were clearly seen.

On May 25, 1893 a magazine called "Nature"

quoted a curious phenomenon being observed
on the wintery cruise of H.M.S. Caroline by
a deck officer on watch. The lights   were
of an unusual nature. Some were spread out.
Others appeared enmass. They bore towards
the north and disappeared about midnight.

Some authorities have endeavored to explain away these sightings as looming mirages
caused by layers of inverson haze, saying
they could duplicate such a manifestation in
their laboratories. Perhaps they are correct in their laboratory deductions, but they
cannot begin to duplicate even in a meager
manner the metal used in these space ships
or the ability of Space Beings to maneuver
them in the way they do and at the speeds
they have been clocked at; all the way from
300 miles to over 18,000 miles per hour.

To correct a mass of incorrect information
given out about space ships, stars, planets,
solar systems, etc., we will endeavor to
give our readers some facts.

These space ships are composed of a kind of
element which does not show on our spectrum,
which is harder than any metal we of earth
have been able to manufacture, yet so light
that two men could lift one of these discs of
50 feet in diameter. That inside of the space
ships they have bunks that one can push back
into place, fitting so tightly into the inner
surface of the craft that one cannot see any
evidence of them being there. Each ship has
its panel board, we will call it, consisting
of the various push-buttons used for the operation of all mechanical objects on board.
Their radar like screens, reflecting mirras,
visa-scopes, visa-phones, radio directional
lights, electro-magnetic mechanism to pick
up light rays concentrating them thru crystals into gyroscopic instruments that create
the waves of light energy referred to before.

ARAMIA

Ray machines for magnetizing or demagnetizing any object, creating of vacuum conditions
or patterns, and for projecting beams of light
force from ship to earth or elsewhere.

At this time these space ships and discs
are setting up landing tubes and broadcasting
centers all over the earth. The landing tubes are about 20 feet in height, composed of
electronic substance, invisible, on which a
discs will settle and remain stationery against a force of wind of other factors. The
broadcasting centers will be of similiar substance, also invisible, but capable of send-
ing beams of energy waves over the earth, along which will travel thoughts of peace, love
joy, harmony and justice, and as humans pick
up these thoughts both during sleep and awakened state they will begin to react thereto
and put into expression such ideas. This will be one way to break up the destructive thought pattern that every nation of the earth
is now spreading upon its inhabitants through
various channels.

The Commander of one of these Space Ships,
known as Aramia, is 5 feet 10 inches tall.
Very dignified. Solidly built, fairly broad
through the shoulders. His hair is long and
golden. The cheeks are pink, eyes large and
blue, his chin strong. He has a very pleasing expression. He wears a tight fitting
tunic of pearl shade silk, with gold and blue
trim, the collar of which is three inches
high, open a little at the throat, with gold
tabs at the ends. On the shoulders of the
tunic are golden epaulets--somewhat similiar
to the "boards" worn by naval officers. He
wears tight fitting trunks of same material,
pearl silk, with a golden zipper up one side
of the calf. His shoes are a soft golden metallic material. While his manner is gracious
it is very commanding. One can feel the magnetic force emanating from his person.   His
command ship is from the Planet Venus. It is

#13

cruising some 75,000 miles above the earth.

He informs me that it is about 7000 feet
long, 500 feet in diameter, with 1500 beings
on board. The skin of the ship looks like
aluminum or stainless steel, reflects a silvery-golden light. It has two entrances,
fore and aft. In the nose is a long panel
board with many push buttons, a view or space mirror, a picture-graph, a sound wave
detector, a visa-scope, a visa-phone, a small radio like instrument which is in direct atunement with the Planet Venus. There
are several seats before this panel board at
which the various technicians sit when the
ship is in operation. We might call these
beings the pilots, co-pilots, navigator,
engineer, radio and sound technicians.

The crew is composed of Venusians from
36 to 42 inches tall. They are well prop-
otioned. Their skin is a light cream col-
or, covered with fuzz-like hair, like the
down on a peach. Their eyes are large and
blue, with hair blonde to golden, brows
fairly heavy, arched, but little. They go
about their work silently, eyes flashing,
at times smiling. Their uniforms are light blue, close fitting, tunics and trunks,
with shoes of the same material fitting tight around the ankles. Many have gold or-
naments on their uniforms, indictive of rank.

The Commander Aramia advises that these
little people are a specific racial type on
Venus, and that a race of little men and women are to be found on Mars as well, while on
Saturn they have a race a little taller but
heavier and more gross in appearance. On
Uranus and Neptune are races of giants. The
little men of Venus and Mars are highly sk-
illed in the handling of mechanical and electrical machinery. You might even call
them wizards when you consider their ability
and knowledge.

This ship is operated in several ways.
One of them is utilizing the cosmic magnetic force in the atmosphere. This energy is
microscopic, white in appearance, and more
explosive than uranium. The ancients called vryil. It is picked up by a series of
coils and converted into power units as the
energy is concentrated thru crystals as they
move thru our etheric belts or atmosphere.
When traveling in outer space from the earth to other planets or between planets they
move along lines of magnetic force at blind-
ing speeds.

The magnetic vortex that extends outward
from our poles in cone shape is several hundred thousands miles in length, reaching beyond the moon, and when these space ships
come into our earth's orbit they come down
thru this magnetic vortex toward the earth
from the north toward the north pole; and
this magnetic force enters the earth from the
north pole, travels thru the earth southward,
into the vortex of the south pole, while the
energy from the south pole vortex travels
over the face of the earth into the north
pole vortex. Therefore, these ships can come
from the moon into the earth's magnetic field
in just a few hours.

By the use of certain instruments they can
create a vacuum around and before the ship,
thus having no friction or resisting force to
overcome. In other words they travel in an
atmosphere of their own creation. There appear to be tubular vents along the outside of
this craft evidently thru which they, by send-
ing bursts of magnetic force on one side or
the other can manouver it in any direction.
Also in this vacuum they can remain stationery

As it is now cruising about 75,000 miles
above the earth many smaller craft report to
and are directed from this source. Smaller
discs can be taken aboard the mother ship by

landing on the top, then lowered inside.

The operators of these craft when report-
ing stand at attention before one of the officers or the Commander and make their state-
ments telepathically. They salute by extending the right arm, palm up, the hand slightly
above shoulder height. When the Commander
gives an order telepathically to any of his
crew one can feel the vibratory effect of this
thought beam, and the force with which it is
directed seems to electrify those to whom it
is sent, as they snap into activity at once.

No maps or charts are used. When a certain area is to be viewed they sweep the area
with a ray beam that travels on the earth
picking up thru a top-like object which is whirling at a terrific speed photographs of ground, outside as well as the inside of buildings, and these are shown on their view or space mirror together with any sounds or conver-
sations. Was astounded to see buildings, plants, airfields, and people working inside of
them, as if televised, and heard the voices
too as they came thru the sound wave detector,
just as heard over earthly radios. When these
voices or tones are converted into picture-
graphs we behold pictures of that which is being said or discussed. These come through ra-
pidly and with clarity. So no matter in what
language the conversation may be in, these
picture-graphs show what it is about.

All thought is universal and convey form,
and when qualified by instruments, such as
this picture-graph, indicate the trend and pur-
pose of the conversation. When we send a tel-
epathic thought to another person it travels
in picture form on waves of etheric substance,
is picked up by our sensorium and readily un-
derstood.

This ship and all others in the fleet are

shielded against any interfering radar waves of earthlings, or other space ships not in harmonious accord with the fleets working in the orbit of the earth. Inasmuch as our earth and solar system is entering the density of the Central Sun Vela, space craft from other solar systems will begin to inspect the earth closer, and unless their attitude is friendly the solar space patrol challenge them at once.

The Commander smiles when the thought is directed to him,
"Are there beings on other planets of this solar system?"
He replies,
"In this vast universe thousands of planets have living beings on them. They do not all resemble earth people, any more than earth people resemble each other in color, height or facial characteristics. Some resemble earth people very closely. Some beings are part human and part animal. These are beings in the lower phases of evolvement. They too fell from grace or a higher status by mating with lower animalistic forms, even as some of the first beings on earth, called the suns of Light, who married or mated with sub-human people."

"Your scientists and astronomers are not quite correct in their deductions and ideas about the planets of this solar system; about other beings not being on them, or thinking there might be only some lower order of living organism existing on them."

"It seems they have decided that according to the analysis of our atmosphere on Venus, by some of their special instruments that there is little if any oxygen and no sign of water vapor. Hence, they believe the surface of our planet must be like a desert, with dust or some strange gaseous formation in our clouds. That the temperature of these visib-

le clouds or cloud layers vary as much as 0
degrees at night to 140 degrees F. in the
day. That the surface temperature would indicate that it might be as high as boiling
point. So without any apparent oxygen, no
water vapor, unfavorable temperatures, there
could hardly be any life on Venus like that
on the earth. They are mistaken. No astro-
nomer thru such instruments as you have on
the earth has ever been able to see our planet itself, nor can they say their instruments
are picking up any direct radiation from the
planet but only from visible cloud layers, and
they are not sure that such do not come from
other sources in space."

"I assure you, that we do have life on our
Planet Venus. Our people resemble earth people very closely. Our cell structure vibrates at a higher rate than does yours, but we
eat, breathe, and digest our foods, though somewhat different than earth fruits and vegeta-
bles, yet they sustain us. We know how to as-
simulate these foods to the best advantage.
We have water and vapor in our atmosphere. We
do not have as many people on our planet as we
had ages ago, but aside from the sub-human group, being part human and animal, and the race
of little people, our people are much more highly evolved than your most advanced scientists
and educators. We do not eat flesh foods of
any kind. In that one department alone we are
far beyond you earth people who are still cann-
ibalistic. When you cease to kill for food,
then you will cease to kill each other.   Why
should any being wish to take the life of a
fellow being, or to eat the flesh of any living
creature. You are still not human, only in
the state of becoming human. You have lost
control of your civilization as well as yourselves, and it remains to be seen whether you
will be able to regain it, without our help.
For in your present destructive frame of mind
you are moving fast toward the destruction of
yourselves, your civilization, and if not pre-

vented might even cause the destruction of
this planet and create such stresses among
the planets of this solar system as to dis-
rupt the whole system.

The earth is the most unprogressed planet of this solar system. Some day through
the purification of the golden-lavender rays
of this Central Sun and other electrical-ma-
gnetic forces from still other sources bill-
ions of your so-called light years away in
space, it will become a bright star in these
heavens. Later it will become a sun, as some
other planets have when its usefulness has
been exhausted."

"Light travels at far greater speeds than
186,000 miles per second. You estimate this
speed as this energy which becomes light on
entering your atmosphere pushes itself from
one point of entrance to another by your instruments. But, you are finding that waves
of magnetic energy, also light, can travel
many times faster than that. The planets of
this solar system are not as far from the earth as your scientist estimate and believe.
The rapidity in which the rays of light energy
travel cannot be estimated for the connections
governing the force that sends light, change.
Your sun is dependent upon the electrical forces centered within it. There are many many
suns, some thousands of times larger than our
sun, but each sun is dependent for its brill-
iancy upon the direct electrical forces of the
spaces that concentrate upon it."

"Space is not a tomb or a vacuum, but is
teeming with life, atomic and electrical, originating so far beyond this solar system that
minds cannot grasp such immensity. Contribut-
ing forces have to be reckoned with. They may
consist of electrical currents which, meeting
produce force. They may also consist of fluids
in the atmosphere. Light travels in ratio to
the condensing power of the receptacle of a

Estralon

particular wave of light energy. Some can receive and register certain speed waves, others
are capable of condensing and receiving a much
higher rate of speed.   Your sun, our sun is
capable of registering a million waves of electrical forces while the moon registers only a
few. Thus the sun becomes the greatest electrical center of light waves in this solar system. Saturn has her own condenser of light as
has Jupiter, while Mars, like earth is indebt-
ed in part to the sun. The sun, however,   is
not a body of liquid fire as the ancients used
to think. The sun is a huge magnet, and the
rapid vibrations from the same generate electro-magnetic waves of energy which you feel on
earth, and when penetrating your atmosphere do
create light and heat. The angle at which these waves enter your atmosphere determine your
seasons.

These Venusians appear to be very highly advanced spiritually, mentally and physically.
Being so pure in their thought they seem almost
angelic. Their love power is intense and blends harmoniously with the vibrations of electrical waves of energy sent out pulsating in all
directions. There are women on board this space craft. The second in command is a woman,
and a very beautiful one too.

As she comes to where the Commander and   I
are standing, he turned to me and said:

"This is Estralon, our second Flight Commander. She has a ship of her own."

She is about 5 ft. 4 inches tall.   Has the
creamest pink complexion I have ever seen on
any girl. These Venusians all look so young it
is difficult to tell their ages.   Her large
blue eyes were like mysterious pools of spark-
ling waters, full of enchantment. She is wear-
ing a uniform not unlike the one worn by   the
Commander Aramia, which reveals a very trim figure.   I imagine she weighs about 115 lbs.
While I could not understand what she is saying

#20

to me in her Venusian tongue, telepathically,
I am able to co-ordinate her delightful musi-
cal voice tones comprehensively.

I noticed the other women on board, all
in uniform, carrying out various tasks, yet
none of them could compare to Estrdon in figure and beauty.

Her love power is intense as I am held in
its radiance. I just seem to melt into her
presence for a moment as her magnetic aura
blends with and overshadows my own. I could
only nod my head as she is presented to me,
as I am still shaken from head to feet by the
dynamic wave of love in which she had enveloped me.

"She will conduct you on an inspection of
the ship and enlighten you further said
Aramia.

As she is talking and indicating the different kinds of ray machines, she stops sudden-
ly and putting a hand on my arm looks at me
again with that tender sweet smile so radiant
and powerful, that I drift momentarily away in
consciousness to a garden filled with a gamut
of beautiful flowers.

"This mechanism is a demagnetizing ray gun
which is used to disintegrate any foreign objects that might interfere with our flight,
such as sizable meteor particles. Also used
to deflect rays from an opposing force, such
as a space craft from another solar system
who does not enter this system in friendship."

It is not shaped like one of the guns you
see on earth on either plane, ship or ground,
but is rather a short tube through which a ray
is projected by oscillation at a terrific rate
of speed, for a considerable distance, which
demagnetizes whatever the beam is directed on.

58

"This mechanism is used to create a vacuum
around our ship which enables it to remain
stationery in this density. We can also use
this form of energy when moving thru space
at high speeds. This pushes aside lines of
magnetic force which would create friction
when crossed. When we travel along lines
of magnetic force we do not need this so
greatly."

Turning to another machine, she says,

"This one is used to expand vibratory rays
of energy which as it increases in tempo is
pushed out in colors, such as red, blue, yellow, reddish-blue, and lavender. The higher
the frequency the more refined the color.
Yellow or golden-lavender is the color you
will observe coming from the Central Sun Vela,
which I shall show you in our space-scope.

"And, this machine picks up the white energy in your atmosphere, concentrates it thru
these highly polished and various shaped crystals, which immediately sets up motion, then
this motion is focused thru several instruments some clockwise, some counter-clockwise,
which enable us to project our craft in the
direction we want it to go, by directing this
colored energy through various jets. Our discs
are not weighed down by heavy loads of fuel,
and when we are moving thru your atmosphere
our bodies are magnetized so they become light
also, thus we are able to move in such tight
circles, at such sharp angles, arcs, and at
speeds that would paralyze your senses."

This machine, as we referred to before,
has a number of various size coils, looks somewhat like copper only of a lighter shade. These
pick up the white substance, vryil, which they
claim is more explosive than uranium, by aten-
nes, and as Estrolon states is concentrated to
some odd shaped highly polished crystals. She
let me look through a visa-scope, focused to a

nth degree, which shows the motion of these
light particles as they move in between and
through these crystals, into other instru -
ments at terrific speeds, hence this energy
is pushed out of various openings around the
craft, setting up a slight humming, showing
various colors, as viewed by earth people.

"Some of our discs have movable rims. A
near central portion moves clockwise; the
exact center being stationary. The other or
outer rim moving counter-clockwise, setting
up what you on earth would term a gyroscopic
balance, enabling the disc to turn at 90 or
180 degree angles, to make tight arcs or circles, to dip and twist if necessary while traveling at speeds ranging from a few hundred
to many thousands of miles per hour, your
reckoning."

"Other discs are controlled entirely from
a much larger disc by beamed energy, like
your radar. These also have movable rims,
and some are without any beings on board, but
have mechanism similiar to the type shown you
before, the (bell pepper type) we will call
it."

"The metals used in the construction of
these disc craft are those which we have on
our planets. They are of a kind that do not
show on your spectrum. They are as elements
fused through an electro process that makes
them so durable, also so light, that we can
construct or form an entire disc in one operation. In this way we can construct a disc
in size from 2 feet in diameter to any size we
desire, say 1200 feet or even 14,000 feet.
We build a space craft, without any sections,
welding, seams, etc., in a like manner, of any
length we desire."

"If your people or leaders on earth were not
so destructively minded we would give you detailed information as to how this is accomplished.

But, that must wait until you learn to live
in peace with one another, then if you of er-
rth have proven worthy of the trust and knowledge we may enlighten you."

I feel like a particle of dust before the
superior wisdom and grace of this young lady.

"Space craft have been making landings on
the earth for many hundreds of years. There
are many references to them in your ancient
writings. They built and used them during the
time the now sunken continent of Mu was in its
height of progression, also used on the cont-
nent of Atlantis, who erected space platforms
in the stratosphere. There are five of these
platforms still revolving around the earth in
its orbit. So you will understand that space
ships are not new to the earth, nor the idea
of space platforms either.

"The first beings on your planet earth were
landed by space craft. They were selected by
the Elders Brothers for their purity, wisdom,
ability and strength from those volunteering
from other planets, not only of this solar system, but from others belonging to what is known now as a Cosmedon or Federation of planets
of other solar systems. Their instructors
were from the planets Mercury and Venus, who
when their period of instruction had ended re-
turned to their respective planets. Other
planets are now being peopled in the same way
now.

"Some planets slow down in vibratory frequency to the point where habitable life cannot
be maintained. Later such planets come to en-
ergized activity again thru the concentration
of electrical waves of light being focused upon them by Exalted Beings in charge of such
activity. Some planets become suns. These at-
tract other bodies to them and form another
solar system.

"Every living creature upon any planet ab-

sorbs and gives off currents or fluids of
electricity. How this is given off and how
absorbed comes under a chemist's observation. But it is an established fact. These
little currents of electricity do not float
off and evaporate like dew, but they reach
out and connect with others, so your atmosphere is charged with electric forces gen -
erated by the connection of the human and
the animal."

"And this is again connected with the greater power beyond your atmosphere, till the
whole becomes so charged with electricity
that it is not only seen but felt, when it
takes the form of 'heat lightning'. The air
has become so rarified by the rays from the
sun that these little electrons blend and
move together in visible form. After exces-
sive lightness and expansion these electrical forces become detached from each other,
concentrate again, then cuts thru the air in
zig zag pattern; the result a thunder storm,
which cools the air. This is what often takes place in the atmosphere around the planet, but far out into space lie the clear and
tranquil ethers, stretching away beyond astronomical sightings and knowledge, intangible
without limits, yet withal real."

"Each planet has its district or orbit in
which it travels held there by magnetic force
lines, and in the ethers each separate group
of planets which you call a solar system re-
volve. There is no record that your earth
has ever left its orbit to travel in the orbit of another planet, tho there is record
that it has been out of its orbit to the point where it wobbled like a crippled being
As it is now spinning on its axis it is changing its position of polarity, which is setting
up a wobbling motion. The time will come when
you will have the star Cephus as your new polar star. By that time the beings on the ea-

rth will have advanced to a great height in
purity, and that is what was really meant
when the Great Teacher Esu, whom you call
Jesus, said to Peter, his disciple, "Hence-
forth, your name shall be Cephus. Upon that (polarity) shall my truth be established
and it shall not pass away."

"Not only do the planets of this solar system have people on them, but your moon has
also, though they have been compelled, due
to its barren condition, especially, the side
which you see thru normal vision, to live un-
ground. They have instruments or machines
for the generating of their own light, heat,
and oxygen, and rarely come to the surface.
They raise their own food stuff, and are in
advance of your civilization. You would be
surprised to know, I am sure, that you have
beings living deep under the surface of your
planet, especially, is this true around your
south pole. These people are known to us as
"Rainbow Beings." They live deep below the
surface and have a type of civilization far
superior to your own, with many intricate
types of instruments for the development of
their own light heat, oxygen and foods. A
number of ray machines have been developed
by them. There are sme other races which de-
terioated. The Rainbow race are a portion
of the old Murian civilization which went underground during the struggle between the Titans and Atlans. Some went in space ships to
Tibet, some to the moon and became marooned
there. Some were able to land on Mars.

"On the far side of the moon, the side never seen from earth, is another race of people. There is vegetation on that side, and
this is the side that many space craft operate from. So earthlings do not get the wild
idea that you can land on the moon and control it and your earth, for you will find other beings, more highly advanced, already on
it, minding their own affairs and not attemp-

ting to control the earth. You of earth still think and act like infants, so we must
bear with you, watching you as you go stumb-
ling along, helping you when you appear to
be having great difficulty, not only to walk,
but to stablize yourselves."

"There is an ancient civilization living
underground with entrances in Mexico, and
not such a great distance from Mexico City.
They often come to the surface and mingle
with the people, but aside from a few mystics, the people of Mexico do not know this,
and they would have a difficult time, if
they did, to locate the entrances to their
underground cities.

"Space craft have landed for hundreds of
years in various parts of your earth where
some of the mystic brotherhoods abide, and
where these underground civilizations still
exist. At every New Age, when the earth
and its inhabitants go thru such great changes, we of space come to your assistance, as
we are in this instance, in great number to
sustain those who have been atuned to the
forces of the light, to work with the great
mystic brotherhoods, and older races, to
keep the earth moving along in its journey
of becoming more illuminated, more wonderful in its expression, more peaceful, more
lovable."

"There are some space craft from the Planet Jupiter also working in harmony with us."

Later I met some of them. These Jupiterians are very dignified and stately. The
leaders are very tall and dark skinned.They
have peculiar facial expressions unlike those of any other planet. Their eyes are large,
soft and very brilliant, dark brown in color.
Their faces are long, one-half longer than
people of earth. Some of them stand seven to
12 feet tall. They are very well built acc-

ording to earth standards. Their women are
very beautiful, graceful and well formed and
are considered some of the graceful of the
planets, even tho they have this odd facial
characteristic. Their skin is very smooth and
radiant. Some of the men wear beards."

One of these Jupiterians, Berasa by name,
about nine feet tall, revealed a great deal
about the life on that planet and gave me an
insight into their deep spiritual natures,
their wonderful ability as creators or rather I should say, exponents of the perfect
type of creation. For it seems, that to Jupiter the other planetary leaders turn for
advice and guidance in cosmedonic affairs.

These Jupiterians are not so very different from those of Mars and Saturn, whom I had
the pleasure of meeting later. They have a
wonderful interpretation of the Creator's love
and power, and express it in their lives.
They have great debating societies where the
law is expounded and questioned--Creative Law,
and a higher understanding of life is thus at-
tained.   The auras of the people of Jupiter
is a wondrous beautiful thing to observe.
Those to whom their friendship is given   may
account themselves as blessed indeed.

The creative mind is very strongly in evid-
enced with them. The power to produce. From
this planet is exhaled the wonderful creative
atmosphere of ideas that flow in greater force
to the earth than to any other planet closer
to them. The power to visualize things, to
conceive new conditions, new environments, new
methods of working out ideas are being inject-
ed into the earth vibration from the electrical work shop of Jupiter, and so they have join
ed with the planetary forces in bringing stron
ger ideas and ideals to earthlings at this tim
For they declare earth people need to be impre
ssed with a greater sense of justice in order
to dissolve the heavy vibrations now crushing

out the Light and Love of the Creator, and to
implant the seed of greater freedom among the
people, and the strength of the New Age Wisdom.

Estralon is saying now, as these ideas are
going thru my mind;

"Upon all planets are beings which were created spiritually free and no being was given
authority to control or bind another individual in its expression. For restraint creates
struggle and friction in striving to be free,
and if this is not correctly directed then
friction becomes violent and destructive. Wit-
ness this on your planet over wide areas.
Leaders in many nations are binding the people in virtual slavery, not only physically,
but mentally and spiritually. Your politicans strive to regiment the voters. Governme-
ntal leaders regiment your youth into military service, into wars created and fermented by
corrupt politicans and munition manufacturers,
all in lust for money and power.

"Even in your worship, your church leaders
subjugate their congregations into ritualist-
ic services and ideas that have no basis of
truth under Creative Law. The Creator is Radiant Light, Spirit, and should be worshipped
as such; not as a god of vengeance, or war, of
destruction, but as a God of Glorious Light,
Love, Peace, Power and everything beautiful.

"All things were created in positive and negative polarity, but each works in harmony
with each other. In energy the negative force
is cold, the positive hot, and you cannot have light until these two are blended together.
Therefore, the negative, now turned toward mis-
creation and destruction must be harmonized
with the positive and LOVE is the motivating
oil to be used to make this operation smooth
and successful.

"Earth people are prone to worship and idol-

ize other individuals, war leaders, politicans, heads of governments, kings, rulers,
church dignitaries, and needed therefore, to
have saviors to lead them into a higher concept of the great creative laws. On Venus
and the other planets of this solar system we
worship the Creative Presence in all forms of
expression and as the authority in all, with
no other standing between us and that Presence. During this New Age you will throw off
the shackles now binding you in ignorance of
this great law and so worship the Creative
Presence direct in all light, activity, and
wisdom. Power and glory belongs only to Him.
Man never did have the authority to usurp it
unto himself. Only to express love in service
unto others."

We had now stopped before the space-scope.
Estralon turned it toward the Central Sun Vela
and slid a colored plate into it, this enabled
us to look at the terrific radiation emanating
in and thru the nine solar systems now moving
into its aurium. The aurium is full of gold-
en light. This is why this Aquarian Age   is
called a Golden Age.

The other eight solar systems, besides our
own, are moving into this aurium at widely different angles in their respective orbits. It
has taken about 100 years of our solar time to
move to the edge of this aurium and during the
next 888 years will move around the Central Sun
in this aurium, and then for another period of
100 years will gradually move out of it and begin its long journey thru six solar light ages
into far distance space, to the outermost limits of its orbit swing; then will begin a long
trip back over six more solar light ages to
the Central Sun. All during this period this
portion of the universe will be revolving aro-
und a still greater Central Sun, and these in
turn around a Medi-Sun so far out in space that

a thousand times greater reflector than the
200 inch one on Palomar could not pick   up
its radiation.

Both Aramia and Estralon state that the
Great Creative Universe around which all other universes are continually revolving is
so far out in space, quad-trillion upon quad-
trillion of our light years could not even
begin to express its distance from the earth.

New solar systems, new planets and stars
are continually being created and taking up
their positions or orbits affixed by magnetic lines of force in these various universes
and cosmedons.   Some planets die out, as the
atomic structure weakens, only to flare up
again ages later as new energy is built up
within it or is focused upon it from sources
far beyond it in space.   Some planets become
suns, some stars become planets, and so life
moves along in varied forms through out the
Creative Universes.

A radiant lavender light vibrates outward
from the center of this Central Sun Vela and
harmonizes with the golden light of its aurium, and thus, as Estralon stated before, the
Golden-Lavender Light is the Light of the New
Aquarian Age.

We turn this space-scope on Jupiter, Mars,
Saturn, Neptune, Uranus, also on far away Pluto, then over to Mercury, Venus, Aspid, Vul-
can, to Sidelius, Nevo, Krona and Absethleon.
Pluto has been mistakenly called a planet. It
is only an asteroid. One of five such broken
off from the Planet Krona, which was partially
destroyed, and whose diameter is now about 15,
000 miles.   This was a most unusual experience.   This space-scope can be adjusted so as to
pick up planets so far out in space that it is
difficult to define or classify them. Some of
the planets we could look right down thru their
cloud canopies to the planet itself.   This must

#31

be how they watch what is taking place on
the various planets, and more especially, the
earth.

The visa-scope is used for more minute
observation at much closer ranges. With this
instrument you could look into the secret
files of an enemy, see what their destructive
war plans are, as well as tune in on some library and read any books desired, without being obliged to go in person. To visit any
museum and see the paintings of the masters
while sitting in your home. More accurately
than if televised by us. Certainly would like
to know how this scope is built. Objectively
it seems to consist of a number of lenses and
crystals very highly polished and arranged in
such a way that they can be focused at either
close or distant range, and as minutely as we
could with a microscope of tremendous power.

This one is set in a square box like aff-
air, and as you look into it you adjust it
from the outside by pressure on certain little buttons. Really remarkable what you can
see with it. You can look thru walls, brick,
cement, iron, glass--into people's bodies,see
how each organ functions. This would be wonderful for locating growths or diseases. Into the brain to observe the thought patterns.
One could readily note whether the individual
had criminal tendencies or not. Examine the
auras of any person, and note the mode of life

She also showed me another instrument, the
use of which on earth would change our lives
greatly. It is called for want of a better
name a "Solar Time Machine". This can be adjusted so one can look into the future and see
what any person, or persons, or nations would
be doing tomorrow, next week, next month, or
ten, twenty or thirty years from now, or even
for a thousand years. It can also be adjust-

ed to look in reverse back thru the past into
the primordial substance where all activity
is recorded and examine accurately what tran-
spired in various parts of the earth at that
period or any other period.

For example she focused it until I was able
to look back at the highest evolved period of
the Murians who lived on the now sunken continent of Mu some 80,000 years ago. Was ama-
zed to see the high state of their civilization. Their beautiful wide expanse cities,
with tall buildings, pyramids, flying machines and space craft. Their solar lighting and
heating centers. The great solar reflectors
that picked up the sun-energy and beamed it
over wide areas in the form of light and heab,
as well as energy. Their many kinds of plan-
es--sled, bat wing, tubular, global, disc,
and many others. We looked closer into their
life activities, their temples, art centers,
ealth centers, industrial centers. The ideas we have today of our progression would
be dwarfed alongside of what I am seeing now
thru this time machine.

I asked her,
"What happened to so wonderful a civilization?"

Estralon adjusted it down to about 25,000
years ago. We see great explosions, whole
cities in ruins, followed by heavy earthquak-
es with outlying portions of the continent
beginning to sink, result of these earthquak-
es. An atomic warfare had started between
the Atlantians and the Murians. Corrupt forces had gotten control in both nations and
continued friction had resulted in an atomic
war. This set off explosions in the gas belts
in the crust of the earth creating earthquak-
es of magnitude, heavy storms and other dest-
ictive activity with Mu sinking.

"Much had been done by certain wise leaders,

mystics, who had established centers in other
lands and sent there those whom they could
trust to carry on the knowledge, wisdom and
life that was being fast destroyed by these
two opposing forces," said Estralon.

"How like the present situation on the earth, with the forces of destruction and construction alined against each other in every nation on earth; and as then, so now, certain
wise men are again picking out thru careful
selection individuals who can carry the torch
of wisdom for the coming generations, placing
them in sparsely settled areas where destruction will not touch them, that the finest shall
not be lost in event the present situation gets
beyond control. At this time, however, these
groups will have the added assistance of our
space visitation. For we are landing and making contact with the many brotherhood, mystic
leaders and some of their chosen workers."

Were our leaders able to look into this
time machine and see what their blundering ch-
ildish acts are creating and what will happen
to the earth, its people, civilization, etc.,
they might at once turn from their wilful ways
into more constructive activity for peace.

Estralon and Aramia both state, almost in
unison:

"We whom you call space beings are not de-
ceived by your window dressing (using your own
language)--peace talks, for we are in possess-
ion of the facts. We know the secret plans in
the vaults of all nations. We know the people
of earth want peace with all other people. We
know that certain leaders do not want peace,
except as they can dictate it. We know that
your group of nations have lost control of the
situation and are not able in their divided activity to bring about peace. Because, within
their own ranks they are not in agreement. We

know the basic principles set forth when this group was organized was not actuated by holy premises, therefore, will not endure any more than your past League of Nations.

"In your own language, earthman, you cannot leave a rotten apple in a barrel and not have the whole barrel of apples affected, even cause the barrel to become rotten too. Your leaders are deceiving no one but themselves, but the sad part of it is they would rather destroy a civilization, even a planet than stand in the light of right principle and action. Therefore, we, as stated, will not stand by and see this earth destroyed as it was in the previous atomic war, even though many of your people hardly warrant better.

"We Space Beings, your Elder Brothers, shall if necessary, use powers beyond your knowledge to preserve the earth and those who will be chosen to become leaders in the New Age dispensation.

"Mark it well, you leaders of destruction, and we know well who you are, we are a patient people, yet we shall move swiftly to purify the earth of your kind when the Supreme Commander gives us the command."

The power that this Commander manifests is so far reaching and great that I am as one transfixed. I give thanks unto these Elder Brothers of Space who have come to the rescue of the children and forces of the Light.

. . . . .o9o. . . . .

In our next booklet "Life on the Planets" we will endeavor to explain how the people on the various planets of our solar system look and live; the kinds of homes, buildings, temples and their cities. Their philosophy and religion.

ADENNDUM TO PAGE 47

Nature **volume 48**, pages 76–77 (1893)

Abstract

DURING a recent wintry cruise in H.M.S. *Caroline* in the North China Sea, a curious phenomenon wasseen which may be of interest to your readers. The ship was on passage between Shanghai and thewestern entrance of the famous inland sea of Japan. On 24th February, at 10 p.m., when in latitude 32°58′ N., longitude 126° 33′E., which, on reference to the map, will be seen to be sixteen to seventeenmiles south of Quelpart island (south of the Korean peninsula) some unusual lights were reported by theofficer of the watch between the ship and Mount Auckland, a mountain 6,000 feet high. It was a windy,cold, moonlight night. My first impression was that they were either some fires on shore, apparentlyhigher from the horizon than a ship's masthead, or some junk's "flare up" lights raised by mirage. To thenaked eye they appeared sometimes as a mass; at others, spread out in an irregular line, and, beingglobular in form, they resembled Chinese lanterns festooned between the masts of a lofty vessel. Theybore north (magnetic), and remained on that bearing until lost sight of about midnight. As the ship waspassing the land to the eastward at the rate of seven knots an hour, it soon became obvious that the lightswere not on the land, though observed with the mountain behind them.

www.ingramcontent.com/pod-product-compliance
Lightning Source LLC
Chambersburg PA
CBHW081200270326
41930CB00014B/3243